Behind The Mask

An Inside Look At Anonymous

Written By: Commander X

Legion Sec Multimedia Unit
Montreal, Quebec - CANADA

Behind The Mask: An Inside Look At Anonymous

Copyright © 2016 by Commander X

Royalties from this book have been donated to Anonymous and other information activist related groups.

Cover Art By: EFG

This work is a true story. Some of the names, locations – and circumstances have been altered to protect the anonymity of those involved.

All rights reserved. No part of this publication may be reproduced, distributed, or transmitted in any form or by any means, including photocopying, recording, or other electronic or mechanical methods, without the prior written permission of the publisher, except in the case of brief quotations embodied in critical reviews and certain other noncommercial uses permitted by copyright law. For permission requests, write to the publisher.

First Edition - Paperback

Published By: Lulu

www.lulu.com

Printed In USA / UK / EU / CANADA

ISBN: 978-1-365-48406-3

Dedication:

This book is dedicated to my hero; Julian Assange, aka *Mendax* - The greatest hacker and information activist in history, and creator of the world changing disclosure and transparency platform WikiLeaks.

Contents

Introduction

Cyber Punks -- 1

Defense Of WikiLeaks – 12

Peace Camp 2010 – 28

Freedom Operations – 42

The FBI Raids – 60

The HB Gary Affair – 73

Creation Of The "Occupy Movement" – 81

Commander X Captured – 95

Operation Xport -- 106

Exile – 155

Post Script

Acknowledgments

INTRODUCTION

Anonymous: The World's Most Secretive Activists

Let me begin this tale by stating for the record: I am Commander X, and I am absolutely a part of the idea known to the world as Anonymous. I am not an outsider looking in, nor am I a former participant. I am not a pundit, journalist or academic expert. I am Anonymous. Everyday, I spend many long hours online working on a slew of current Anonymous Operations. And this isn't a hobby, or a part time endeavor - this has become my sole life's work. And more than even that, Anonymous is my culture, my lifestyle - and the philosophical context for my entire worldview. It is this fact that I believe sets this work apart from the many other books that have cropped up lately on the subject of Anonymous.

The challenges in writing this book were numerous. First and foremost, I produced this work while on the run from the FBI, NSA, CIA, CSIS, RCMP, various police departments in the USA and elsewhere - and at least three death squads from around the world. As I complete this book, I have entered political exile in Canada and I am in hiding. In addition to this rather daunting hurdle, I also found it nearly impossible to lay down the multitude of responsibilities I have in various operations, actions - and projects within Anonymous. I did not have the luxury of taking a "working vacation" from cyber-activism in order to work on my writing.

Finally, there is the challenge of the subject matter. When I began this project many years ago, I was immediately faced with one conundrum; how does one publicly tell the story of a movement that is so secret that its participants will only appear publicly in mask? How do I share the details and inner workings of the many wonderful things Anonymous has done in this world without seriously endangering the people who are a part of this idea called Anonymous? And as I sit here in exile from my own country due to some of those activities, and indeed hunted and stalked by those who would have me dead for the work we have done - it is a weighty question and no small matter.

If I screw up, people could be imprisoned, they could be hurt - they might even be killed.

This of course begs the question that many Anons asked me during the preparation of this work for publication; why bother? Why write this book at all? The answer is twofold. First, I firmly believe that Anonymous is one of the most powerful forces of our time. Having been a part of Anonymous, I feel very strongly there is an obligation to the historic record of mankind to relate our story from the inside - to explain to the world and posterity how and why we did the things we did.

But beyond this, there is an obligation to contemporary society. There can be no argument that Anonymous is having an incredible impact on the events unfolding in our world today. As such, we have a responsibility to account for our actions and the great power that fate and political forces have bestowed upon Anonymous. For it would be hypocritical of us to demand, as we have, transparency from the governments and corporations that rule our world - and not offer up transparency ourselves. Now some would say this is an impossible contradiction, anonymity and transparency. But this is not actually a contradiction. One enables the other. By tending to our personal anonymity and making that bullet proof, we enable ourselves to safely open up our actions to the scrutiny of the world and history. It allows us to act as one and be accountable as one, while keeping us all safe from the oppressors.

And so I have entered upon the quixotic and nearly impossible task of relating the tale you now hold in your hands. It is a story of secrecy, shadows - and those who began as simple activists and found themselves at the center of one of the most powerful movements in the history of mankind. Throughout the preparation of this manuscript, I have taken great care to protect those who risked everything for the simple dream that we might live in a better world.

Where necessary, I have altered the names, locations — and circumstances of the story in order to protect those who are not only a part of Anonymous, but in many cases my dearest friends. In order to offer the reader a glimpse into the thoughts, fears, motivations - and hopes of an Anon, I have chosen to tell this story using the first person narrative.

When it comes to my own participation in these events, I have attempted to be as accurate, transparent, open - and honest as is humanly possible. With regard to historical accuracy, I have tried to research as best I can the events I am about to relate. I have discovered great differences in the narrative I have so often given in media interviews, and the actual facts and dates. So hopefully this book will set some of the record straight, and help me give better interviews to journalists in the future as a side benefit.

Ultimately I have done my best. I did not live my life with the recording of it in mind. I kept no diaries, I rarely logged my chats in IRC or other channels. I have my own memory and what ever material was archived on the internet to work with. Any errors or inaccuracies are solely my fault, and the reader has my apology for them.

In the end my goal was not to create a history book of Anonymous itself. This has already been done, and by those who were involved far longer than I was in the meme. Probably the best example for those looking for a thorough historical review of Anonymous is the documentary movie "We Are Legion: The Story Of The Hactivists" produced by Brian Knappenberger. What I have tried to do, with all the love in my heart, hope in my soul - and intellectual capacity I possess; is to bring the reader on a journey inside the mysterious and wonderful world of Anonymous. Hopefully, I can give you just a small glimpse *Behind The Mask*.

www.CommanderX.info

Commander X - April 2, 2013 - Quebec City, Quebec - Canada

ONE

Cyber Punks

"You only need two things to be a world-class hacker: A computer and a cool pair of sunglasses. And the computer is optional."
~~ Commander X

Tuesday - March 25, 2008 approx. 2:30 PM EST - Cambridge, Mass. USA

It was one of those cloudy, windy and bone chilling days so common in the Boston area this time of year. Winter can cling tenaciously, and spring can be hard pressed to make a true stand for a good month. As I walked down the dirty sidewalk with filthy lumps of snow in the gutters, through what is commonly known in the area as the "student ghettos" of Cambridge between Harvard University and MIT - I was distracted and tired. Occasionally, as they almost always did - the frost or root heaved broken pavement of sidewalks that seemed to never get the attention of the City of Cambridge would seem to rise up on their own and trip me from my dazed and exhausted reverie. Fifteen years of walking down this street, and I still could neither navigate the blighted sidewalks, nor could I ever seem to find the house I was looking for. Perhaps it was because they all seemed to look exactly the same. Often, I would not realize I had passed it until I saw the "Now Entering Somerville" town line sign. Then I would curse, turn around - and literally count seven houses back, feeling like a moron.

   Today wasn't that bad, thankfully. I came upon the ramshackle century old house, and sighed. Originally all these houses, which could have been shit out from a giant house making machine they looked so much alike - were all single family dwellings. But during the Great Depression, poverty forced nearly all the owners to illegally sub-divide them into multiple apartments. The vast majority were two story dwellings with two units per floor, and often one in the basement as well. The more desperate property owners even adding a tiny barely habitable unit in the attic. While each house at some point in its beknighted history had been painted a different color, they had all since faded to dullness so that on an overcast day like today they all looked grayish yellow.

During the summer months the smell of garbage and piss was so strong it could make you gag. The worst part though was the garbage itself. Since each house was so completely sub-divided, and because each unit was crammed full of young students attending either Harvard or MIT - the garbage situation was truly deplorable. Some houses would literally have refuse piled completely around them like a ring around Saturn, awaiting that one day a week when the City of Cambridge *might* come and pick it up - *if* someone remembered to drag all the filthy crap to the edge of the street.

It was in the basement of one of these dubious dwellings that a tiny under ground political group known as the Peoples Liberation Front had located its headquarters for the past thirteen years. I pushed open the metal gate at the side of the house and crabbed sideways towards the rear of the property, trying desperately not to touch the mountains of garbage piled along the side of the building. It wasn't that I was all that clean myself, but I feared injury if one of the huge piles were to avalanche down upon me. Popping with audible relief into what can only euphemistically be called the "backyard" of the property (approx. 50 square feet of compacted dirt and dog shit) - I pulled out my key to the door that led to the basement. The stairs were steep, and the bottom had this strange way of seeming to come up at you suddenly. Many a late night, high or drunk - had found me sprawled on the basement floor from a graceless entrance to what we jokingly called "The Dungeon". Immediately my nostrils were assailed by the strong smell of burning marijuana and brewed coffee.

The basement was divided into three rooms. The first we referred to as the "Living Room", and its furnishings consisted of an ancient and thread bare sofa so filthy it was impossible to tell exactly what color it had originally been, and which was currently serving as the bed of Tobey - a relatively new PLF Member who was crashing in HQ until he could find more suitable living quarters.

A coffee table, piled two feet high with assorted litter, beer cans and bottles -

and perched precariously on top a rolling tray with roaches, cigarette butts, rolling papers - and approximately a quarter ounce of what looked like some rather cheap marijuana. One overstuffed and equally filthy armchair, and three relatively new folding chairs completed the accoutrements of what served as the recreational area of HQ. Debris of every conceivable type littered the floor, now added to by most of Tobey's worldly possessions - such that there was no way to navigate the room without constantly clearing a path in front of you with your foot.

But what new visitors immediately noticed, most being unable for many minutes to keep from studying - were the walls and ceiling. Every square inch was plastered with concert posters (mostly Grateful Dead), protest fliers and handbills, comics torn from this or that publication - and hand drawn art, mostly political in nature. Most new comers never even saw the rest of the room at first, being completely captivated by this insane collage which in a strange way documented the history of the PLF in a way that no book or movie ever could.

I tossed my grubby day pack and laptop case onto the sofa, after searching in vain for a place to set it on the floor - and lit a smoke. It was then that it hit me, something was wrong. Instead of the usual blaring live Grateful Dead show screaming on the stereo in the corner, there was silence. And in place of the usual cacophony of shouted voices competing to be heard over the music, there was only hushed tones emanating from the next room. There was definitely something seriously amiss. I took another long drag off my cigarette, and steeled myself - and walked into the work room which we called "The Lab".

Tobey and Allison were seated at computer stations, of which there were four total on benches along two of the walls. This room was in considerably different condition than the "Living Room" as Commander Adama, the Supreme Commander of the PLF - demanded that it be kept clean and orderly. Along a third wall was a bench containing two photocopiers, a printer, telephone and fax and various accoutrements for underground publishing such as staplers, hole punchers, scissors etc. Standing in the center of the room behind Tobey and Allison was Adama himself - his back to me as I entered.

Adama was an impressive man by all standards. At six foot six inches his head practically touched the ceiling of the basement. Two hundred and eighty pounds of very solid muscle filled his trademark denim jeans, turtle neck and leather flight jacket. A neatly trimmed full head of steel gray hair completed this imposing man. By any standards he was a good looking man, although other than a few whores he and I shared on a mission in the Caribbean - I never knew him to have a woman in his life. He was a charismatic person the likes of which they write epic tales about.

A born leader, who was never wrong. You wanted Adama to tell you what to do. "Tobey, I thought I gave you an order to clean up that pig sty in there" I said as I entered the room, hesitant as I could feel the tension in the air. "Sorry X, I'll get to it later" Tobey muttered without turning from his computer screen. "That's *Commander X*, Tobey, and you will do it now - that's an order" I snapped. Adama turned to me and half smiled. He had been getting on me lately to be more assertive with the crew, who had been slipping in discipline recently. Tobey especially had been an issue. Young, talented and cocky - he more than earned his place in the Peoples Liberation Front.

But he had never quite grasped that while we are Anarchists, we were also a militia. He would eventually be jailed in Italy for drugs, and be cast out from the PLF in disgrace - but not before making many heroic and incredible contributions to our group. His back stiffened in his chair, and then he rose and tried to exit the room without looking at or acknowledging me. I gently but firmly reached out my hand to stay him. "The appropriate response is 'Yes Sir' Tobey, and I thought you said you would have a place to live last week" I said firmly. Still refusing to look me in the eye, he looked over his shoulder to where Commander Adama had stood - but

Adama had taken a seat at the computer Tobey had just abandoned and was typing away on the keyboard. Finally he turned to me "Yes Sir. I will be out this weekend *Commander X*" he said with a smirk and walked past me into the next room.

I let out a deep sigh. Sometimes this job sucked, and guys like Tobey did not make it any easier. I lit another smoke and walked up to the space in between where Allison and Adama were seated at computers. Kicking a milk crate out from under the work bench, I sat down between them. I leaned into Allison, she always smelled so good - and said in a low voice: "You shouldn't be coming here anymore it's too dangerous".

Commander Allison had recently taken a job with the US State Department in hopes that the PLF could infiltrate that branch of the US government. It was an extremely dangerous idea that she and Adama had cooked up after she graduated with a degree in political science. Upon entering their employ, she was forced to sign a document stating that she agreed to be spied upon by US authorities for the rest of her life. She leaned over and kissed my ear "I know" she whispered.

I sat up straight, blew out a long trail of smoke and said "so my comrades, what exactly the flaming fuck is going on?". Both of my friends sat up straight on either side of me and regarded me with smiles that at once exuded warmth and conveyed consternation. "This is what's up X" Allison said and tapped her keyboard once bringing up a web site. The same site was already up on Adama's screen as well. I regarded them both with a slightly puzzled look, and then leaned in to examine the site as it appeared on Adama's slightly larger monitor.

As I could see from the browser's address bar, it was the Epilepsy Foundation of America home page. But something was wrong with the page. On it was a large animated gif that strobed in a hypnotic and almost psychically disturbing fashion. I recognized this image at once from a computer article I had read somewhere.

Studies had shown that this image, and others like it - had the capacity to actually induce seizures and even coma in certain individuals who were susceptible, especially epileptics. The page had been "hacked", defaced as we term it in the business. "Who in the fuck would do something like this?" I asked breathlessly, almost stunned to speechlessness by the utter depravity of the act. Allison smiled and turned back to her computer and started typing. I turned to Adama as he leaned back his head and let out a chuckle. He looked down at me sitting on my crate "Ever hear of a group called 'Anonymous'?".

"Anonymous?" I said as I wracked my brains trying to tease out a vague recollection from recent media reports. Allison tapped my shoulder and pointed to her screen. On her monitor was a recent online news report detailing the ongoing protests against the Church of Scientology. "You mean the crazies with the Guy Fawkes masks? You have got to be kidding me, right? This is some kind of joke?" I asked in dismay. In my mind at that time Anonymous was a crazy ass science fiction based cult who had gone to war with another crazy science fiction cult, like a looney toon cartoon where two complete idiots proceed to pummel each other into smithereens.

But while I knew plenty about Scientology, I knew next to nothing about their mask wearing nemesis - Anonymous. "They are not a cult, nor are they crazy" Adama said as he leaned back and lit a cigarette. "They are a techno-hacker group, just like us" he explained as he exhaled a stream of smoke towards the ceiling. "Bullshit. Not like us, we would NEVER do something like this. These fuckers are pure evil if they did that." as I pointed at the site still up on Adama's screen. "Perhaps" Adama said laconically. "Of one thing I am certain. They are powerful, and getting more so by the day. I want to know everything there is to know about them. And I want you and Allison on the inside.

You two are going to become members of Anonymous" he turned to me and took a drag from his cigarette. I turned to Allison hoping for some support, but she was smiling this big shit eating grin and even giggling. "Ah shit, this is really going to suck" I said as I reached for Adama's pack of cigarettes.

Tuesday - April 14, 2009 approx. 8:00 PM - Cambridge, Mass. USA

Now I knew I was starting to get old, as I walked into the work room of HQ the new guy whose name I couldn't even remember turned to me from his computer.

"Commander X, sir - Commander Adama would like to see you in his office *sir*!" the kid said with just a little to much enthusiasm. Dressed in full camo khakis, and with all the proper PLF insignia sewn on his shoulder and breast (the only person I have ever known to wear the full and official PLF uniform on a daily basis), this young man's enthusiasm was just a wee disturbing. "Right" I muttered. "Uhmm, at ease" I said, at a loss for how to deal with the full martial treatment. Shaking my head and wondering how we could get some of this kid bottled up and feed it to Tobey, I gently knocked on Adama's office door and entered without waiting for a reply.

Adama's office was the third room of our basement HQ. Whereas the "Living Room" was usually trashed, and the "Lab" in a state of clean yet creative disarray - Adama's office, like Commander Adama himself - was always immaculate. The only sign of anything amiss was piles of books, folders, magazines and papers piled high on the four corners of a large steel work desk. As I entered, Adama was sitting at his desk, head in both hands and rubbing his temples methodically. He didn't look up as I sat in the chair across from him. "You okay old man? You don't look so good" I asked gently. He slowly raised his head and looked directly at me, blankly at first.

I stared back, studying him. Deep lines were beginning to crease his face, and there were disturbingly large bags under his eyes. I had known Adama for over a quarter of a century. We met during the anti-apartheid movement in the mid-eighties. He and I, together with four others including Commander Allison - founded the Peoples Liberation Front in 1985. While no one knew Adama's exact age (or much of anything about him for that matter), he had to be almost 70 by my guess.

A smile slowly crept across his face. "I'm fine X, just a little tired" as he reached into the top drawer of the desk and pulled out a bottle of pills. He popped the top, tossed back a few - and washed them down with the last of his coffee. Handing the mug across the desk, he said "get me a refill, will you? Get yourself some too, we have some things to discuss". I shook my head and grabbed his coffee cup and went over to the coffee maker in the corner. A fresh pot had just finished brewing as I came in, and I proceeded to make up a couple of cups just the way we both took it. You spend 25 years working with a man one thing you learn, and that's how he takes his coffee. As I worked with my back turned to him, Adama said: "I am going to promote Isis to the rank of Commander". I paused, and looked back at him over my shoulder. "She is solid, Adama - but she is also very young" I said.

Isis was a relatively new recruit, having been a member of the Peoples Liberation Front for a little over a year. She was 20, and drop dead gorgeous. With a perfect figure and long flowing blond dreadlocks falling to her waist - when Isis entered a room you took notice. She was a brilliant hacker, politically savvy - and in every way a genius. She was also very loyal to the movement in general and the PLF in particular.

As I turned with the two steaming mugs of java in hand, Adama said simply: "She is ready, and we need her". I set the mugs down on his desk and sank back into my chair across from him and shrugged. "Fine, it's your call - you're the boss" I replied.

Adama took a long pull of his coffee, set it down and opened the side drawer on his desk and pulled out a pipe. He lit it, took a long hit - and handed it across to me. For the next ten minutes we shared "the sacrament" in silence. Finally he spoke. In a somber tone he said: "I need a favor X". I looked at him steady for a moment, and then replied: "Well, that's a first. You should know by now all you have to do is ask". "I need you to do a ground mission" he stated plainly. I cocked my head and looked at him for another moment. "Since when are ground missions 'favors' boss?" I asked him. He looked away into the distance and said in a low voice: "This is different, it's...personal. A favor for an old friend". I lit a cigarette and took a long drag. This was a different Adama sitting here, that was for sure. Always strictly business, the business of non-violent revolution - Adama didn't do or take anything for himself. Ever. "Talk to me. Where is this 'mission'?" I asked. "Santa Cruz" Adama replied as he tossed a folder across the desk.

I stubbed out my cigarette and picked up the folder. Written in Adama's meticulous handwriting on the cover was simply "Santa Cruz, California". I opened the folder. It contained dozens of newspaper clippings, along with computer printouts of news stories and some editorials. For the next few minutes I read through them in silence while Adama sipped his coffee and smoked a cigarette. The long and short of it is that Santa Cruz, a place that all of the founders of the PLF were familiar with having visited the city many times - had a dark underside.

The city and county officials had been on a crusade for two decades to try and stem the burgeoning tide of homeless and street people who were flooding the city in massive waves. At times this repression had been positively dystopian, with cops dressing in gray coveralls and military boots while off duty - and under cover of darkness attacking the homeless camps and beating the street people.

One had died, and six cops had been caught, fired - and convicted. Teenagers in the city had formed a "goon squad" called the *Troll Busters*, and even had tee shirts with a logo. They were finally disbanded when one day, from a foot bridge over looking a river bottom - they fired a homemade mortar round into a homeless camp below. It went on and on. Increasingly repressive laws being passed to try and make life as miserable as possible, with the goal of causing the homeless to simply leave the city. Police harassment of the street people was a matter of public policy. There was even a law that made it illegal to cover one self with a blanket anywhere in Santa Cruz out of doors during certain hours of the day. It was a pogrom, no doubt about it - and serious violations of basic human rights were a daily occurrence.

I finally set the folder back on the desk and looked up at Adama. "I don't get how this is 'personal' boss. This seems like a pretty standard human rights op, and frankly one that we probably should have done awhile ago." I stated. Adama rubbed his chin, and stared off into the distance for a moment, and I swear for the first time since I knew him I saw a tear form in his eye, then he said: "You are perhaps correct, X. But my motivation is still personal. There is an old friend, from a very long time ago. He is a homeless man in Santa Cruz.". I thought about that for a second, then said: "So? Give me a dossier and I'll find him and get him out of there". Adama again looked into the distance. It finally occurred to me, he was staring into the past - a long way into the past.

Finally he said: "That won't be possible. My friend died. Last week. Of hypothermia. They found his body on the San Lorenzo river bottom. He didn't even have a blanket. He was hiding from their draconian 'sleeping ban'. I want vengeance. That's why it's personal, and you don't have to go if you don't want to".

I digested this for a moment. Then I looked him in the eye and said: "Fine, I'll do it. But I have two conditions. I want this to stay between you and me, this idea that it's personal.

I'll get your revenge for you, that I promise - but as far as the others are concerned this is a standard human rights action and nothing more". Adama looked up and smiled, raising his hands in mock surrender: "Fine, fine. And the second condition?". I thought about sunny Santa Cruz, with its radicals, anarchists, its pirate radio station and beautiful beaches and mountains - then I looked up at Adama. " I want to bring Isis with me" I said with a leering grin.

TWO

Defense Of WikiLeaks

"In this sense, WikiLeaks has become the 'great equalizer' - encouraging people across the globe to be wary of authority and those seeking high political office." ~~ Aljazeera

Sunday - May 2, 2010 Noon - Greyhound Rock, California USA

The view off the cliff tops was breath taking. I tried always to stop and take a breather at the newly installed benches for the lazy tourists. I would climb out of the over-stuffed (and extremely heavy) mountain pack, and sit quietly and smoke a cigarette. It was already looking like a hot summer ahead. In the distance and up the road some I could hear the sounds of industry, Big Creek Lumber Company - which dominated this section of the coastline and quite far inland as well. It was the last of the old family owned redwood mills on the west coast, and a perennial target of the Earth Liberation Front out of Santa Cruz. An ancient and gnarled old man by the name of Ludd McCrarry owned what amounted to a small kingdom out here where the Santa Cruz mountains began their long march inland from the sea.

I took a moment to catch my breath, reflecting over the past year in Santa Cruz. I never dreamed during that last meeting in Cambridge that I would still be in Santa Cruz, and still struggling to find a way to exact vengeance for the untimely death of Commander Adama's friend. Although things may be changing fast in that regard. If only I had known back then that would be the last time I would see Adama alive. If only...

I sighed heavily, stubbed out my smoke - and shrugged into the insanely heavy mountain pack. I still had one hell of a climb ahead before I could relax with a hot cup of joe and a pipe full of kind buds. I was trying to get a week's worth of supplies into my camp up on the ridge-line so I could hang out and work on "the girls". Twenty-six of the most gorgeous sativa/indica mix plants the likes of which you could only grow in the black earth of the Santa Cruz mountains. I was looking forward to the peace and quiet of the forest.

The past week in the city had been hectic, and last night was a truly dark one in Santa Cruz - where the annual May Day protests had turned ugly and degenerated into a riot in which some fifty-thousand dollars worth of damage had been done to the downtown area on Pacific Avenue.

Local Anarchists were being blamed by the media and authorities, and once again the FBI were roaming the sunny streets of Santa Cruz. With ELF active on the Campus, and the local pirate radio station "Free Radio Santa Cruz" agitating as always, the feds had plenty to keep them busy in politically active Santa Cruz.

The news from "home" was not much better. A group of hackers and information activists called WikiLeaks and headed by the former hacker known as "Mendax" and now known to the world as Julian Assange had recently published a short movie called "Collateral Murder" which documented the wanton killing of unarmed civilians and even journalists in Iraq. My sources within the US government confirmed that there had been a massive breach of both the .mil and the State Department classified data bases, and that WikiLeaks was now in possession of a vast trove of secret documents belonging to the government of the USA. The shit was about to hit the fan, as Commander Allison had put it.

I sighed deeply as I dropped the mountain pack in the camp. I threw up my arms and stretched and looked out over my little domain. Up here it seemed like the "world" of humans was a million miles away. Perched upon the very first ridge-line of the Santa Cruz mountains, the "Camp" was divided into two principle parts. The first was a cluster of shelters built under a copse of 75 year old Douglas firs. The second part was an open sunny grassland area I called the "Glade". As I turned towards it, I could easily see the over two dozen three foot tall marijuana plants taking on the late evening sun sparkling off the Pacific. I smiled, even with storm clouds of revolution on the horizon of human history - life was still all good.

Thursday - July 15, 2010 approx. 2:30 PM PT - County Courthouse Santa Cruz, CA USA

The encampment/demonstration on the front steps of the County Courthouse was barely ten days old, and already it had grown far beyond the expectation of the original organizers. Dubbed simply "Peace Camp 2010", it was an occupation for social justice that pre-dated the very idea of the "Occupy Movement" by a good year. The camp had a festive air, we had managed to hold off the cops and we were feeling pretty good. All of us, that is - except the original organizers of the protest who began all this on Independence Day. Sitting on the grass in a semi-circle in front of me were Ed Frey, a local attorney who had provided the critical component of the port-o-john on a trailer, Becky Johnson a local activist and blogger - and Robert Norse a local homeless activist and radio personality. Robert's show aired twice a week on the local pirate station Free Radio Santa Cruz, and he had lately taken me on as a co-host. None of them knew that I was actually Commander X, member of the Peoples Liberation Front and part of Anonymous. That is something they would find out much later, when the FBI finally managed to catch up with me.

"Look, I know you guys are burned out - but there's no reason to fold up the tents here." I said as I lit a cigarette. "Go home, get some rest. I will secure the port-o-john at night, and set up more media stuff during the day." I continued. Becky sat there, disheveled and obviously discouraged. In her dirty hands she held a cardboard sign she had made that said "We Won!". I had to hold myself back from going off on her, and screaming what the fuck did we win? The homeless were still being hunted all over the city like animals, the laws were still in place. Yes, Ed had managed to temporarily flumux the county leaders with some legal sleight of hand that kept them from trouncing Peace Camp 2010 into dust, but we hadn't won shit. And the cops would eventually crush us, it was as inevitable as the sun rising in the morning.

I pressed on "The three of you have done an amazing thing here. You organized what may well go down in Santa Cruz as the longest running, largest - and most effective protest in this city's history. But you're exhausted.

I have decades of experience in organizing occupational protests, going back to the 80's and the Anti-Apartheid movement. I can handle this. Step back and rest, get out of the spot light for a bit. I will take the heat for awhile" If only I knew that this was a decision that would eventually lead to my being man-hunted by multiple police and intelligence agencies across two countries.

Friday - December 10, 2010 approx. 6:00 PM PT - Pacific Avenue Starbucks Santa Cruz, CA USA

I hate Starbucks, I really do. They are useless corporate fucks who don't give one shit about anybody or anything except profit. But with a registered Starbucks card you could get endless free refills, and they had free WiFi. I was waiting patiently in a special chat room designed by the PLF called the Ajax Server for my boss, Commander Adama. Ajax had been designed by our star programmer, Isis. Isis had long since left me in Santa Cruz. Being young and full of energy, she had quickly become bored with a mission that had stagnated into what seemed like an endless quagmire. She was basing out of San Francisco now, and she had come down and got herself arrested twice at the end when after sixty days the cops had finally crushed Peace Camp 2010.

The sound of gently tinkling Tibetan bells announced the arrival of the Supreme Commander of the Peoples Liberation Front.

Commander Adama: Greetings X. How are you?

Commander X: I'm okay, the "girls" came out great. I gave most of the harvest away at Peace Camp 2010. How are you?

Commander Adama: I am well, X. We have a lot to discuss. Are you in a safe place?

Commander X: I am, what's up?

Commander Adama: First, I have made an important decision. We are coming out. We are going to bring the Peoples Liberation Front out of the shadows. I have Isis working on the web site now. It's time for us to open up and become transparent to the world, and start recruiting online.

Wow.

I paused for a good two minutes. For over a quarter century the PLF had been one of the most secretive and underground groups in the world. This was going to change everything. Absolutely everything.

Commander X: Adama are you sure? This is dangerous shit you're talking about my friend, even the FBI doesn't believe we exist - you can't put the jinni back in the bottle once you do this.

Commander Adama: I am sure. Isis will have the site ready in the next couple of days. I want you to start keeping your eyes open for people we can trust to bring in. Soon, things will heat up - and we won't be able to trust anyone. The window to openly recruit good people will be small.

Commander X: And where exactly should I look for these "recruits" Adama?

Commander Adama: That brings me to my next point. Today Anonymous took down the PayPal website in what may well be the largest crowd sourced online protest in the history of the Internet. They did it in defense of WikiLeaks, to protest the bank blockade of their donations portal.

Commander X: Yeah, I know - I read about it. So?

Commander Adama: The Peoples Liberation Front is going to join forces with Anonymous. I already have people here at HQ attacking their next target, and Isis and Tobey are working on a secret weapon for you. I want you to join their IRC server and help them any way you can.

Commander X: Jesus Adama, are you serious? We are going to join with Anonymous, like *allies*?

Commander Adama: They *are* allies. You will see. Just trust me X, okay?

I know this is a lot for you to digest, but this is the road to an amazing future. The events of the next week will forever change human history.

I stared at the blinking cursor. I thought back over the last twenty five years I had spent doing everything this man told me to without question. What he was proposing was the most dangerous move our group had ever made. There had to be a good reason.

Commander X: Okay. Give me the IRC server address....

An hour later, on the AnonOps IRC server in channel #OpPayback over 5000 cyber activists from all over the world had gathered:

trivette: TANGO DOWN TANGO DOWN TANGO DOWN visa.com !

I checked in my browser, and sure enough - the bastards were offline.

I brought up the program I had running called the LOIC, which was short for Low Orbit Ion Cannon. The LOIC was basically a simple web site stress tester, a standard tool of every IT used to test the capacity of web sites. But dressed up in a fancy interface to make it "feel" like a sort of weapon. It was steadily firing a stream of request packets at www.visa.com. And all over the world, approximately ten thousand other people were doing the same thing. I was using the screen name "PLF" on the IRC server.

PLF: Shit man, we did it!   Target is DOWN West Coast USA!

Tux: Someone tweet that shit. There's a pirate pad url in the topic for anyone who wants to help write the press release.

Absolem: Guys, this shit is on CNN right now! `

The_N0: This is amazing.

PLF: Hey everyone, it's not just CNN. They got us on NBC, CBS...shit pretty much every MSM network in the world is reporting this. We are even on Aljazeera!

ISIS: I think we just made history. Again.

tFlow: Couldn't have happened to a better bunch of assholes.

Tux: According to NBC VISA says this is costing them a million dollars a minute this close to Christmas.

PLF: Good. That's how you hurt these mother fuckers, hit them in their wallets.

Absolem: Hey, what does PLF stand for anyway?

PLF: Peoples Liberation Front. We are an underground resistance movement. We are here to help, to join the fight.

trivette: Hey that's kind of cool, actually.

BarrettBrown: Okay, just got off the phone with NBC. How is the press release coming? We should get that out soon.

Tux: Hey Barrett, saw you on Aljazeera tonight, good job bro.

BarrettBrown: Thanks. We should organize a black fax and/or E-Mail Bomb soon. That would turn up the heat.

tFlow: Lulz. Yeah, well looks like they're pretty toasty already.

At that moment I got a PM, or private message - from Absolem. I clicked on the tab to chat back channel.

Absolem: This is incredible. I can't believe we just wiped out VISA.

PLF: I know, I never imagined this many people would get involved. Look at that, 5000 people in one IRC channel. It boggles my mind. NBC called it the largest online protest in history.

Absolem: And there is more out there firing, the HIVE counter says almost 10,000. They just aren't joining the IRC.

PLF: Wow you're right. I was so busy I didn't even notice. That's a fuck lot of people.

Absolem: So...I was curious about your group. The Peoples Liberation Front you called it.

So here it was. The first person in history to openly inquire about us. My first instinct from decades of secrecy was to lie and get the fuck out of there. But I had my orders. I took a deep breath and prepared to tell a total stranger what until then I hadn't even told my own wife while I was briefly married.

PLF: Well, you've probably heard of our sister organizations ELF and ALF. In one sense we resemble them, in that we have an extreme definition of non-violent resistance. But where ALF focuses on the fuzzy things, and ELF the green things - we focus on people. And we tend to work with technology, using it to assist protests and movements. We are sort of...the intelligence agency and tech support of the underground. We were founded in 1985, so we have been around awhile.

We have a hierarchical organizational structure, unlike ALF which is a hydra and ELF which is cellular. We are sort of...a cyber militia. Our leader is called Commander Adama. My name is Commander X. We will have a web site out in a couple of days that will explain better, I will get you the link when it's done.

Absolem: Man, dude that is so cool. I would like to be a part of something like that. I have dreamed my whole life of being a part of something like that.

PLF: Well, let's set up a meeting with the boss. I think that can be arranged.

Absolem: :-)

Tuesday - December 14, 2010 4:00 PM PT - Roasting Company Cafe Santa Cruz, CA USA

The attacks on the various financial institutions that had cut off services to WikiLeaks was now well into its sixth day. The number of Anonymous participants was beginning to decline as the FBI ratcheted up its rhetoric about how illegal the protests were, and the targets were getting harder to take down as their IT departments began fortifying their servers against the DdoS attacks. It had definitely been one of the most exciting weeks I have ever spent in cyber activism. And we were all going through changes, inner changes. Our ideas about power, about what was possible in the world, about what one could achieve with this amazing new tool called the Internet - all of these were transforming us so fast it was one epiphany after another for a week. And for myself personally, I was forced to confront my ideas about this movement called "Anonymous". In the past two years I had gone from thinking of them as a totally nihilistic gang of cyber punks to finding them only a mildly annoying distraction on the information activist front. Up until this week, I had still not completely embraced Commander Adama's view that they were the most powerful force for resistance and change in human history. But this week had changed all that. Working with so many brilliant hackers and cyber activists under the flag of Anonymous had led me to believe that my friend was probably correct in his assessment. More than that though, I felt like I had actually become a part of this idea called Anonymous. I found myself being defensive against their online critics, bristling at the cyber-trolls who slandered them. And I found that I not only felt a deep love for this movement called Anonymous, but the people in it as well. Just goes to show how much can change in just a week.

It was also during this week that I would meet the man who would become my dearest friend in Anonymous. Barrett Brown was a well published author and self described propagandist for the movement. As one of the original members of the shadowy forum called /b/ on the image board known as 4chan, he had actually witnessed the birth of Anonymous in 2005.

Barrett was what they called in Anonymous a "name-fag", a term of derision which basically meant that he had chosen to forgo his anonymity. In Barrett's case he had done so voluntarily in order to act as a sort of un-official spokesman and media liaison for the movement. When a news outlet wanted an interview from someone in Anonymous, and refused to accept some masked person with a funky hacker name and morphed voice - we sent Barrett Brown to deal with them like a lamb to the slaughter. It was a truly thankless job, trying to represent the collective.

Barrett was constantly "trolled" by those in Anonymous who criticized everything from the contents of the interviews to the fact that he even gave them. "Fame-whore" and "ego-fag" were some of the nicer names that were hurled his way. And virtually every word out of his mouth on the record was parsed and torn apart by the self appointed "meme police" within Anonymous for the slightest departure from what was considered the official philosophy or principles of the movement.

But Barrett Brown understood that if Anonymous was to have a place in the media dialog then someone had to step forward and fulfill this role. And he was great at it, fulfilling his duties with brilliant intelligence, an insider's grasp of the facts and a biting wit that belied Barrett's complete disregard for all so called "authority" or those in power. And for the world at large, Barrett Brown was people's first glimpse behind the Mask of Anonymous.

Our goal all day had been to bring down the web site of MasterCard. But unlike the earlier victories of the week against giants like Amazon, PayPal, VISA and even the Swedish Prosecutors office (taken down at my insistence for having intervened against Julian Assange in a court hearing in the UK) - the beast was not going down easy. While we had certainly slowed the web server down considerably, we had failed to take it down completely. And with the whole world watching, failure for Anonymous was not an option.

The media had come to paint us as an invincible and implacable force, and that gave Anonymous great power. But in order to keep that power, we had to basically always win - especially on the big battles where the whole world's media were focused on us. I turned my attention back to the IRC channel as over 2000 cyber-activists attempted to turn the MasterCard web site into a smoking crater in cyber space. Just then I got a PM from PLF Commander Isis.

ISIS: Hey X, how are you? I have a little surprise for you. A gift from me and the crew back home.

PLF: I am okay, what have you got?

ISIS: Remember the "secret weapon" Adama mentioned last week? It's ready for deployment.

PLF: Yeah well your timing is perfect, what is it? Give me the specs.

ISIS: Short explanation, we used some of the war chest to rent out 500 high end servers created thousands of virtual machines and installed modified HOIC's with special booster packs tailored for the Op Payback targets. We tied them all together through a central interface and they can all be fired simultaneously from the web interface. Our estimate is it would equal approx. 30,000 individual activists firing the standard LOIC.

PLF: Wow.

ISIS: :-P

The HOIC was short for High Orbit Ion Cannon.

Where as the LOIC fired a single stream of data requests at a single target, the HOIC was capable of firing in theory at over 250 separate targets and producing many thousands of streams per target. You could also load special "booster packs" tailored for individual targets. These are special scripts that would take advantage of a particular server's vulnerabilities. It was an incredibly powerful cyber weapon, but bear in mind it was still nothing more than a dressed up web stress tool. Having thousands at our disposal that could be fired on command from a single interface was devastating. Too devastating.

As the implications of this new toy the PLF elves had cobbled together for me set in, I came upon a moral and ethical conundrum. This new super-weapon was in essence a botnet. While it did not consist, as most botnets did - of computers hijacked from innocent and unsuspecting victims, it was nonetheless a giant botnet. The whole point of a DdoS attack is that it was essentially a cyber sit-in. The power of the protest was directly proportionate to the number of people willing to step forward and join in. In a weird sort of way this felt like "cheating".

PLF: Ok send me the link to the control panel.

It looked pretty much like a normal HOIC embedded in a web page. But I knew that it was linked via the standard hive IRC based protocol to 10,000 actual HOIC's on high performance virtual machines with T1 broadband connections located all over the world. It was already set up for tonight's target, MasterCard. The moment of truth was upon me. This is what command decisions are all about. I checked the main Op Payback channel. They were still furiously struggling to down the target, and the reporters embedded with us that night were beginning to ask pointed questions about whether or not we would succeed in actually dropping MasterCard. I sighed and typed into the channel:

PLF: Behold, the might of the Peoples Liberation Front!

Then I hit the fire button. It took exactly 5 seconds to turn MasterCard.com into a cinder. Now *that's* a cyber weapon. Back in the IRC channel it was tFlow who caught my cryptic remark and realized what it must mean.

He did a target check and began furiously typing into the channel:

tFlow: OMG TANGO DOWN TANGO DOWN MasterCard.com is fucking TOAST!

I smiled to myself. I did my own check, sure enough it was gone. Another giant slain by Anonymous that week.

PLF: Target - DOWN West Coast USA.

BarrettBrown: Well done PLF, well done. Much respect.

One by one, people from all over the world reported in that MasterCard was down from their location. It was a complete and global take-down. I had just crossed a line. I was now fully a part of this idea called Anonymous, there was no going back. "Guess I'll have to buy one of those stupid Guy Fawkes masks now" I muttered to myself as I stepped out of the cafe to smoke a cigarette.

There have been so many milestones in my three decades as an activist. Being there at the end when Apartheid fell, battling the CIA for nearly ten years, the defense of Napster in "Operation NetShield" together with the Chaos Computer Club and the Cult Of The Dead Cow - all of these helped to define the person and activist I am today.

And that week, working with Anonymous to exact revenge for the injustices perpetrated upon WikiLeaks and its brilliant founder Julian Assange was yet another turning point in my career. I felt rejuvenated. I felt like I was twenty again. More than anything, I felt hope. Hope that activism really could make a difference still, and that it didn't need to take years to accomplish change.

And I felt the first inclinations of power. Not only group power, but personal power. In retrospect it was also a turning point for Anonymous. Operation Chanology, the fight against Scientology - had welded them into a political and social movement. And taking on and doing significant damage to a powerful and dangerous enemy had given that movement confidence. But Operation Avenge Assange had shown Anonymous that tens of thousands were willing to join with them, to fight beside them. And with those numbers came power, because as with any movement it takes numbers to make a difference. In one week, Anonymous had at least doubled in size - with no end in sight. A new IRC channel called #OpNewBlood was created just to train new Anons in the basics, and even weeks after the Op Avenge Assange attacks ended it was still training an average of a hundred people a day to be a part of Anonymous. With ever increasing speed, Anonymous was morphing into a giant cyber-army - whose command and control centers were coffee houses, student hang-outs and hacker-spaces all over the world. But as Anonymous began to contemplate how it might best wield this new found power, I and the PLF had our own problem to deal with.

The past week had been bad for the local protest, Peace Camp 2010. The residual occupation - which had moved from the County Courthouse to Santa Cruz City Hall, had finally been crushed from existence by the brutal local police. And the County Prosecutor had announced her intention to charge several of the key activists involved in its organization, including attorney Ed Frey and a local activist named Gary Johnson - who had become a dear friend of mine during my stay in Santa Cruz.

But the past week had given me not only an idea which was bubbling around and taking shape in my mind, it had given me a new ally. A giant headless dude with the power of a cyber-god called Anonymous. Myself and the PLF had fought beside and earned the respect of Anonymous, and what's more - we had come through in a pinch. With their help perhaps, just maybe - I might exact a small amount of that revenge I came to Santa Cruz to obtain for Adama.

THREE

Peace Camp 2010

"An individual who breaks a law that conscience tells him is unjust, and who willingly accepts the penalty of imprisonment in order to arouse the conscience of the community over its injustice - is in reality expressing the highest respect for the law."
~~ Martin Luther King, Jr.

Thursday - December 16, 2010 approx. 5:00 PM PT Roasting Company Cafe Santa Cruz, CA USA

I sat there simply staring at the E-Mail message I had completed over an hour previous and re-read many times already. It was addressed to over two dozen local and state media organizations and reporters. It was by far the most audacious and provocative missive I had ever penned, and I was hesitant to hit the send button.

Dear Media –

At exactly noon local time tomorrow, the Peoples Liberation Front and Anonymous will remove from the Internet the web site of the Santa Cruz County government. And exactly 30 minutes later, we will return it to normal function.

We are doing this to protest the un-just and political prosecutions of the "Peace Camp 8", who are being maliciously persecuted for the crime of organizing and participating in peaceful protest against the massive human rights violations against the street people and homeless of Santa Cruz. We will issue a further clarifying statement immediately after the take down of the web site.

If you reveal this knowledge, either through your respective media outlets or to law enforcement - before Noon tomorrow, you will be black listed from the media lists of the PLF and Anonymous and receive no further communiques from either group.

SINCERELY -- Commander X
Field Commander Of The Peoples Liberation Front

Never in the history of the PLF had we ever claimed credit for a cyber attack, never mind pre-announcing it prior to the fact to the media. It seemed to me to be simply insane, but Commander Adama had assured me this was to be the new norm. Anonymous always took credit for their actions, and often pre-announced them. This was peaceful protest, electronic civil disobedience he had insisted. And the best way to conduct these "cyber sit-ins" is to give the media a heads up. I had already spoken with some of the Anons I had met the previous week during Operation Avenge Assange and we would have the fire power we needed for the take-down tomorrow. Fuck it, I hit the send button. Let the chips fall where they may. I closed out my E-Mail window and brought up my Nmap scanner which I had trained upon the servers of the City of Santa Cruz and specifically those belonging to its barbaric and brutal police department. The data was interesting, and there might just be a way to get inside and poke around. It might take me all night, but I was hopeful.

Friday - December 17, 2010 approx. 11:00 AM PT Starbucks Pacific Avenue Santa Cruz, CA USA

I was neck deep in the servers of the Santa Cruz City Police Department. With approximately one hour to go before the attack on the county servers, I had handed off command of that attack to Commander Adama so as to concentrate on my attempt to penetrate the police servers. I knew that Absolem was in the channel for the county attack, and that he would be trying to impress Adama. It had been nearly two straight weeks of daily sometimes hourly cyber attacks on someone, somewhere. Things were getting a bit surreal. And the feds were making big noises in the media that they were going to shut Anonymous down.

The tweet scrolled by at exactly noon. The Santa Cruz County website had been made into a smoking crater in cyber-space. The first local media reports on the attack were already being published, and the entire city was abuzz with the news. I sighed, rubbed the bridge of my nose and went for the day's third latte.

This shit was all getting a little close to home. It somehow seemed important to begin accepting the possibility that this might not be my home for much longer. Was this it then? Was I doomed to be this weird cyber-warrior from now on? Were coffee houses and hack spaces to be my command and control centers? And here before my eyes we had struck one small blow for these poor and desperate people being hunted by their own government like animals. It was impossible to know the taste of power in the face of power and not feel good about it.

I was exhausted. And I had to finally admit that I was not going to get past the final layer of defenses on the SCPD servers. I could see the file structures, but couldn't seem to touch them nor get my root kit to stick on the drive. It was hopeless. There was still about ten minutes left in the "attack" on the Santa Cruz County website. I sighed and flipped up the tab with the command and control chat channel and logged in. I immediately got a private message from Commander Adama.

Commander Adama: How did it go with the SCPD servers X?

Commander X: I failed. I was so close but they have some sort of new security I simply don't understand. I couldn't get at the files we wanted, nor could I gain root control.

Commander Adama: Don't let it disturb you X, you did your best. Make notes on what you found in case we need them in the future.

Commander X: Already done. So, how did our first recruit Absolem perform today?

Commander Adama: I put him on firing detail and his HOIC jammed almost immediately. So I detailed him to keep an eye on media reports and to act as a liaison with the AnonOps IRC to get us more guns. He is doing well, very enthusiastic.

Commander X: Excellent, I have a good feeling about him.

Commander Adama: As do I. Well, it's almost time to give the cease fire order. Commander X, will you do the honors?

Commander X: Happy too boss.

I closed out the PM window and brought up the main chat pane. In the chat there were a dozen or so members of the PLF and trusted Anons. Absolem was busy shooting links to the various local media reports which were already pouring in even though the brief half-hour attack wasn't even concluded yet. We had certainly made a scene in this small beach community.

Commander X: Good afternoon everyone. Thank you all so much for helping with Operation Peace Camp 2010. Absolem, if you would be so kind as to be at the ready to give the cease fire order in the AnonOps IRC.

At precisely 11:59 PM PT I typed into the chat...

Commander X: Please cease firing on our target now. Absolem, tell them in AnonOps.

Exactly two minutes later everyone reported that the Santa Cruz County website had returned to normal functionality. At that exact moment, two detectives from the Santa Cruz County Sheriff's office entered the Starbucks. "Shit" I muttered to myself. It was time to find somewhere else to be.

I quickly typed my good-byes and a last thank you into the chat and began packing up my things as calmly as I could manage. My heart was fucking pounding. As I exited the Starbucks on Pacific Avenue, there directly in front of me less than ten yards away and standing in the street was Phil Gomez a reporter for the local ABC affiliate and a cameraman with their backs to me interviewing the Santa Cruz Chief of Police about the take down. It was time to get the fuck out of town.

Heart still pounding, I made my way as calmly as I could down the street and towards the Santa Cruz City Library. I sat outside on a bench, facing City Hall and smoked three cigarettes in a row. But my job was not done yet, far from it. I entered the library and found the farthest corner I could, and got out my laptop. I fired up the E-Mail and sent out the following message to all the local media:

Peoples Liberation Front Statement To Santa Cruz

DATE: December 17, 2010

The Peoples Liberation Front is now, and has from its inception been a NON-VIOLENT, pacifist group of freedom fighters. Never have we as a group or individually EVER been so much as accused of an act of violence. No one anywhere has anything to fear from our group, that is unless they are evil, criminal - or tyrants.

Those have much to fear from us and they DO fear us. For over two decades we have used information and technology to battle in a non-violent way to win justice and freedom for everyone.

Today's action, as the County spokesman pointed out - did no harm. No payloads were injected, no data bases were violated - and no hardware was damaged. And that will continue to be the case, I assure everyone. But there will be more attacks if the Peace Camp 8 are prosecuted.

The Op Commander for today's action was Commander Adama, our leader. He led the troops who joined with us for today's action from our secret Operations Center in Massachusetts in the USA.

At precisely 12:30 PM Pacific Time the cease fire order was given. At 12:32 PM Pacific Time the Santa Cruz County Web Site returned to normal function and became available globally to all our listening nodes.

Again, I urge you all to join us. Go to our site, download a Lazor - and stand for Human Rights, human decency - and freedom in your community. The PLF is here to help, not to harm. And finally, I call upon all those who hear this - help the Peace Camp 8. Please, write to your government leaders, go to City Council Meetings - dig deep until it hurts into your pockets for cash so they can defend themselves properly.

We actually have faith in your court system.

We are NOT trying to influence your judicial system in any way.
Our research indicates that their judge will be more than fair. They appear to all have adequate representation.

But the defense fund is essential, please look to your hearts and give - some of these folks are desperately poor - and the defense looks to be elaborate and expensive.

We do wish however, to influence the prosecutor. We believe that this is a malicious prosecution that is politically motivated. We did not need to hack anything to figure that out - we just read your local newspaper archives. So, please - if you are listening prosecutor, it's Christmas for gods sake - drop these rotten and illegal charges against these humble and innocent and terribly brave street people. FREE the Peace Camp 8.

I sighed deeply as the "message sent" box popped up. This was all getting very real fast. As much as I wanted to jump on the coastal bus and get my ass the hell out of town and return to my mountain camp, I still had one more chore to fulfill. One that was even riskier than anything I had yet done.

But the local media had been whipped into an absolute frenzy by the cyber assault on the county servers, and there was one last thing I could do to stoke the attention to the plight of the Peace Camp 8. I had already told the Santa Cruz Sentinel, the local news paper - that Commander X of the Peoples Liberation Front would be calling in to the local pirate radio station Free Radio Santa Cruz during that evening's radio show hosted by local homeless advocate Robert Norse. In the meantime though, I felt the need to get out of sight and I was exhausted. I packed up and set out for the public park that ran along side the San Lorenzo river for a nap.

Later that night, in the Coffee Roasting Company cafe - I fired up Skype and voice morphing software and did my call in interview with Robert Norse on FRSC. The interview was brief, and plagued with technical problems. I was relieved when it was over, and I made my plans to get the hell out of town for a much needed break from civilization. As I was boarding the bus the next morning, a headline in the Santa Cruz Sentinel caught my eye. Looking around in either direction, I bought a copy and stuffed it in my pack just before boarding the bus north.

Cyber Hackers Shut Down Santa Cruz County Website Briefly

December 18, 2010

SANTA CRUZ -- A little-known Massachusetts-based group that says it will fight for freedom at all costs is claiming responsibility for shutting down the Santa Cruz County government website Thursday.

The site, which is the Internet home of the district attorney, the sheriff and other county offices, was largely inaccessible to the public for about 30 minutes shortly after noon.

County officials acknowledge that someone from the outside interrupted the site's operation. They do not know who it was.

The Sheriff's Office is investigating and the FBI has been contacted, county officials say.

Information Services Director Kevin Bowling explained the problem as a brief interruption for the viewing public but said no internal systems or information were compromised. "It's just a nuisance," he said. "They're not causing any damage. They can't get in to do anything."

The Peoples Liberation Front, whose website details a mission of fighting for global freedom using "cyber warfare," sent an e-mail to several news organizations Wednesday announcing it would launch a cyber attack on Santa Cruz County the next day.

The e-mail said the attack was a response to the unfair prosecution of Santa Cruz demonstrators in the so-called Peace Camp 2010 last summer. The Peace Camp was a protest of a camping ban in the city of Santa Cruz and a gesture of solidarity with the area's homeless community.

Thursday's cyber attack came a day after two of the Peace Camp protesters were arraigned in Santa Cruz County Superior Court on charges related to illegally staying overnight at the County Government Center as part of the protest. Four others face similar charges.

A handful of domestic terrorism experts contacted by the Sentinel say they are unfamiliar with the Peoples Liberation Front. But the group's website says it has interrupted Web operations in many places, including major credit card companies. The group also says it's been helping mount online attacks in support of controversial media outlet WikiLeaks.

In an e-mail inquiry to the group, an Anonymous member going by the name "Commander X" told the Sentinel the group became interested in the Peace Camp because another Anonymous member knew a participant in the protest. The group declined to say which local demonstrator it knew and said its actions Wednesday were performed unbeknownst to that person. Local attorney and Peace Camp organizer Ed Frey confirmed that local demonstrators knew nothing about the Peoples Liberation Front or the cyber attack.

County officials say they've taken steps to prevent a similar breach. They acknowledge, though, that such attacks, which essentially aim to overwhelm the visitor capacity of a website and force traffic to crawl, are hard to stop.

Monday - December 27, 2010 approx. 7:00 PM PT   Roasting Company Cafe Santa Cruz, CA USA

I had received word from street activists that two FBI agents had been asking questions about me for days in Santa Cruz. I had been out at my mountain camp, recuperating from the hectic activities of the past month in town. Needing supplies, and not sure exactly what to do next - I had been forced back into the city where I found out about the federal dragnet for me almost immediately. I had spent the day on the San Lorenzo river bottom, hiding and sleeping. Finally I decided fuck it, what ever is going to happen - let it be.

The first hint that something was wrong is that I couldn't login or connect to my VPN. Almost immediately after that, I saw one Santa Cruz police officer coming in the front door of the coffee house as another came in the back way. I was trapped, I was V&. They were upon me fast, and even as I reached to shut the power off on my laptop to protect the encrypted partitions - one officer lunged across the table and grabbed my laptop by the screen and pulled it away from me. The two SCPD officers they sent to pick me up were partners. Officer Wallace and Wilson. While Officer Wallace hated my guts, Wilson and I had a grudging relationship of respect.

"Get up Doyon" Officer Wallace said with a growl. As I stood up, Officer Wilson injected himself between us. Gently he led me from the cafe while Officer Wallace began packing up my backpack and computer. I was quickly cuffed and placed in the back seat of a waiting police cruiser. As we began wending our way through the city, it became apparent that I was not being taken to the County Jail - which was the normal routine. Having been arrested in Santa Cruz more times than I can count for my political activism, I was extremely familiar with the process.

"Where are you taking me?" I asked, a little nervous at the change in pattern. Officer Wallace simply gave an evil chuckle. Officer Wilson looked up at me in his rear-view mirror from the drivers seat and said simply: "There are some men who have some questions for you, we're going to the station".

At the Santa Cruz main police station, I sat in the cruiser with Officer Wilson while Officer Wallace began bringing all my possessions into the station. I looked up at Wilson. Over the years, he and I had developed a bit of a rapport. Although we were both clear on the lines that divided us, there was a sort of mutual respect and honor between us. "What the fuck is this all about Wilson?" I asked. "Hell I was hoping you could tell me Chris" Wilson replied turning to look at me.

"All I know is I am doing someone's bidding" he said with a tone of disgust in his voice. He got out of the drivers seat, opened the passenger door and helped me out of the backseat. He checked my handcuffs, which were behind my back. "Are they okay?" he asked me. "Yeah, they're just dandy Wilson" I said with a sardonic smile.

Officer Wilson chuckled and led me into the station. I was taken into an interview room. "Just sit there" Wilson pointed at a chair "two men have some questions for you". "Feds?" I asked. "I told you, I don't know - they didn't tell me Chris. But I would say that's a good guess." Still standing I looked Wilson in the eye and said: "Look I have been cooperative, and if I am going to be here awhile how about giving me some dignity and cuffing me in the front?". Officer Wilson shrugged and said: "Sure Doyon, you've earned that at least". He took off one hand cuff, brought it around front of me and re-cuffed me. I sat down to await these mystery men and their questions.

About ten minutes later, the door swung open and two men walked in. These were not your average G-men for certain. Dressed in grubby jeans, dirty gray hoodies and wearing equally filthy sneakers - these guys looked more like college rejects than feds. But each carried a *very* large laptop case, and that was the giveaway. They were federal cyber-crime agents, no doubt about it. They went to the other side of the table and reached for two chairs preparing to take a seat. I raised my cuffed hands to stay them. "Can I see some identification gentlemen?" I asked. They paused, glanced at each other briefly - and as one reached into their back pockets. The two produced standard issue FBI badges and ID cards. I examined each one carefully, making note that indeed both these men were from the FBI's cyber-crime division based out of San Jose, California. Satisfied, I nodded at them and settled back into my chair. The two agents once again reached for the backs of their chairs to pull them out and have a seat. Once again raised my hands to stop them. "That won't be necessary gentlemen, you won't be here long enough to get comfortable. I want my phone call, and my attorney.

And I won't be answering any questions." I said firmly with a bit of a smile. The two FBI agents once again looked at each other, shrugged and proceeded to depart the interview room.

A few hours later, at the Santa Cruz County Sheriffs complex across town - I sat in another interview room awaiting my local attorney and fellow activist Ed Frey.

Ed, who was one of the original founders of the Peace Camp 2010 protest at the courthouse was an older gentleman in his late sixties - slim, handsome and tall and with a stylish white beard and ponytail. He entered the interview room and immediately put his fingers to his lips and looked around as if to say "the walls have ears". Ed sat down and laid some paperwork the sheriffs had given him on the table. He leaned in close across the table that separated us and in a hushed but insistent tone I spoke into his ear: "You need to get me the fuck out of here Ed, and quickly - and we need to get my computer back from SCPD before they turn it over to the FBI idiots." I whispered. Ed nodded and leaned back enough to look me in the eye. "I signed the paperwork, you'll be out of here in two hours. But the property room at the SCPD doesn't open until morning, nothing we can do about your computer until then. I'll meet you there in the morning and we'll get your stuff back."

Tuesday - December 28, 2010 approx. 9:00 AM PT Police Station - Santa Cruz, CA USA

We sat in Ed's beat up and ancient pickup truck in the parking lot of the Santa Cruz Police station. It was raining. We sat in silence waiting for the property room to open so I could reclaim my backpack and hopefully my laptop which was seized by SCPD when they grabbed me for the FBI the night before.

On the way there I had told Ed pretty much everything, and he now fully understood the urgent need to retrieve my laptop. Finally, we got out of the truck and jogged through the rain into the side door of the station where the property room was located.

After filling out the paperwork and cooling our heels for what seemed like a painfully long time, the property room door opened and a cart was wheeled out into the waiting room - pushed by none other than a smiling Officer Wallace. "Shit, not this asshole" I muttered under my breath as both Ed and I got to our feet to examine my belongings.

I quickly looked my mountain pack over, reached for my laptop case and looked inside. I looked up at Ed and shook my head slightly. Ed looked up at Officer Wallace and said: "My client seems to be missing a laptop computer, Officer". Officer Wallace smiled a positively evil smile and handed Ed a bright orange sheet of paper. "Your client's laptop and cell phone were seized as evidence by the FBI cyber-crime division" he said with a chuckle before turning to leave.

When we exited the police station, the rain had stopped - although it was still overcast and a bit muggy. I hurled my mountain pack and now empty laptop case into the back of Ed's pickup and lit a smoke. I rubbed my eyes and inhaled deeply on the cigarette. I was exhausted. I had spent a restless night camped out in Ed's office to stay out of the rain and so we could get an early start to the police station. I climbed into the cab of the pickup and Ed cranked the engine over. "So, what now Chris?" Ed asked. "North, to my mountain. I need to figure out what the fuck to do now" I said in a resigned tone. Although the answer to that question had been forming itself in my mind for a day now.

As we made the short drive north to the base of my mountain home, I explained the situation to Ed. "Basically, if the feds have my computer they have everything they will need for an indictment on violation of the Computer Fraud and Abuse Act" I said. "I am fucked" I moaned.

"What are you going to do?" asked Ed. I shrugged. "Run. Run like hell" I turned to him and said. "I will go underground, try to stay free as long as I can and keep fighting the bastards any way possible" I told him. We pulled into the round out at the base of my mountain, and I climbed out of the cab of the truck. "Chris" Ed said as he handed me a small bundle. It was forty dollars wrapped around a small bag of marijuana. I looked up at him. "Good luck my friend, give them a good run" he said with a smile. As he drove off, it started to rain again. -------------------

The world around me at that time was changing at breathtaking speed. Although no one could completely foresee it, we were already hurtling towards the twin phenomenon of the so called "Arab Spring" and eventually the "Occupy Movement". The world of cyber-activism was also morphing and maturing, finding new tactics and causes it could effect.

The WikiLeaks organization had profoundly effected the landscape of the free information movement, and struck fear into the very heart of many governments in the process. Anonymous was flexing its new found power and casting about for how best to apply it. The whole planet was indeed approaching an obvious tipping point, a cathartic moment in human history - and it felt strangely like we cyber-activists were somehow at the tip of the spear. While I couldn't anticipate the details the future held, I could sense the ominous presence of these world-changing events.

Obviously in my own life I had also reached a moment of flux. I was about to become a fugitive, being man-hunted by the FBI. Somehow in the brief space of a month it had all become deadly serious. I knew as I climbed the mountain in the slow drizzle that day that my life would never be the same. If only I had known how completely surreal it would be for me before it is said and done. Things weren't just getting serious, they were getting strange. And the real weirdness had yet to really appear.

FOUR

Freedom Operations

"First, in the name of all Tunisian people - I want to thank Anonymous. Anonymous were the only ones to help us. Anonymous has blocked all government websites of the Tunisia government because the Tunisian government has blocked our Internet access so we may not get information. Thank you Anonymous! We want to let you know that you have found new allies and that there are many more people living in oppression." ~~ Speaker (Holding A Guy Fawkes Mask) - Rally After Tunisian Revolution

Friday - December 31, 2010 approx. 8:00 AM PT - Waddell Creek, California USA

It was a breezy and cool morning, fair skies and sun. I stood in the center of my camp up on the ridge-line and looked about slowly, taking in every detail of my home. My heart was heavy beyond anything I had ever felt. Something told me I would never see this place again, and I was filled with the grief of it. At my feet was my "road kit", my mountain pack and laptop case. So this was it. I knew that at the bottom of the mountain was Route 1, and an adventure the likes of which I could not imagine. No longer would I have a place to call home, no more familiar friends and family every day. From now on, I would be hunted like an animal by the federal government of the USA - or worse I would be caught and spend a goodly amount of time in prison. My life would be spent on the run, in hiding - and in constant fear of capture.

And make no mistake, the FBI was closing in fast on Anonymous. Soon, they would pounce - and things would get ugly fast. I wiped away a tear for the home I would never see again, hoisted my pack onto my back, slung my laptop across my shoulder - and began picking my way down the ridge towards the highway. Every foot of the way down the mountain that day I drank in. The tree where the humming birds lived, the stump in the trail where I knew the squirrel liked to hide on sunny days - this was "my" mountain and I was going to miss it something terrible. Finally I reached Route 1, took one last look up the ridge-line - and stuck out my thumb heading north to San Francisco and whatever history had in store for me.

Saturday - January 1, 2011 approx. 6:30 PM PT - Coffee To The People Cafe San Francisco, California USA

It was good to be back in San Francisco. It was always good to be in San Francisco, in my opinion. It was the first day of a brand new year, and for the first time I could remember - I had absolutely no idea what the next year would bring. But my gut told me it was going to be interesting. After all, it was beginning with me being on the run from an FBI hacking investigation and eventual indictment. With G-men and Cyber Crime Agents hot on your trail, it's doubtful life will be boring. It was beginning to sink in that my life would never be the same again.

Coffee To The People was a classic revolutionary cafe in the Haight-Ashbury district of San Francisco that had been the breeding ground for many movements and revolutions over the decades. The place reeked of rebellion. Even the tables had old protest flyers and literature laminated into their tops. Today found me online with a group of Anons in an IRC chat room having a wide ranging conversation centered on trying to define some sort of direction for this movement called Anonymous. As more activists began joining Anonymous in the wake of the Op Avenge Assange attacks, there was a general push to "do something". But the conservative elements who ran the AnonOps servers and infrastructure were reluctant to launch new Ops willy nilly. Getting tired of what seemed like a circular debate, I PMed Barrett Brown to try and get some sensible insight.

X: Greetings.

BarrettBrown: Good evening X, how are you?

X: Not bad, considering I am beginning the New Year on the run from the FBI. How about you?

Barrett Brown: I am good. I suspect they will come for me eventually as well. Stay safe.

X: Where is this all going? What do you think should happen next?

There was a long pause. I'll never know whether Barrett was thoughtfully considering my question, distracted by another conversation - or just doing some drugs. But when he finally replied his answer was probably one of the most prophetic things ever uttered in Anonymous.

Barrett Brown: The mid-east. Watch the mid-east very closely.

I had no reply. I was new in Anonymous, and I didn't know if Barrett was referencing something obscure or something that was common knowledge. But in just under 48 hours I would have my answer, as a tiny country called Tunisia became the focus of a Global Collective of hacktivists called Anonymous - and the Arab Spring was born....quite literally before my eyes.

Sunday - January 2, 2011 approx. 10:30 AM PT - Coffee To The People Cafe - San Francisco, California USA

For those wondering how Anonymous begins a major Operation, it usually starts with righteous indignation bordering on group outrage. As I logged into the AnonOps IRC server, there was plenty of anger flowing in the main channel. The focus of this anger was once again WikiLeaks related, but with a bit of a twist.

It appeared that the tiny mid-east nation of Tunisia had blocked access to the WikiLeaks website to try and thwart some particularly un-flattering Diplomatic Cables being leaked with regard to the dictator Bin Ali and his tyrannical government. Anonymous is a strange group of activists.

On any given day governments around the world are slaughtering hundreds, maybe thousands - of innocent people. But block information, censor the Internet in the slightest - and Anonymous was ready to burn the world to the ground over this offense. Almost as soon as I logged on, Barrett Brown pinged me in PM and told me to go to the Op Tunisia channel. While there seemed to be some debate over starting an Op for Tunisia in progress in the main channel, apparently the decision to proceed had already been made. I flipped open the tab and joined the channel. As I entered the channel, Barrett Brown acknowledged my entrance rather dramatically.

Barrett Brown: The Peoples Liberation Front is here and presenting arms for Tunisia!

X: We'll do our best. What exactly is the plan at the moment?

The first goal of those in the Op Tunisia channel was to try and circumvent the Tunisian government censorship of WikiLeaks and other web sites, thus making those banned sites available to those inside Tunisia.

This is not actually a terribly complex problem to solve, involving the set up of a series of proxy servers and some DNS slight-of-hand. The real trick was in getting the simple instructions on using the procedure into Tunisia and disseminated among those who can make use of it. To that end, people not involved in setting up the technical stuff were tasked with harvesting both E-Mail addresses and fax numbers from Tunisian cyber space. The work went slowly, with a great deal of it being accomplished by small groups in PM back-channels.

There were Tunisians in the channel, and they were helpful in many ways - from testing solutions to assisting in the harvesting of contact data and the spread of what was becoming known as the "Anonymous Care Package".

Within a year, Anonymous would begin preparing generic "Care Packages" in advance crafted for various potential hot-spots and regions of protest. What started that day became, as so many other things over the next few weeks would - a sort of "standard operating procedure" for cyber-insurgency.

Word of our efforts was spreading quickly within Tunisia, and at least some independent media were actually reporting not only the damning information on the WikiLeaks web site - but how people could circumvent the government censorship and access the information for themselves. And it wasn't just Anonymous scrambling, the WikiLeaks crew was reaching out for translators and setting up a special section of the web site just for the Tunisians. Then, as dawn began to light the streets of Tunisia - people began to pour from their homes by the hundreds of thousands. Somehow, word of concrete proof of the corruption of the Bin Ali regime had reinvigorated the waning protest movement which had begun some two weeks previously with the self-immolation of a fruit vendor named Mohamed Bouazizi - enraging the general populace and bringing renewed hope to those Tunisian activists who thought it possible to actually topple the dictator completely and usher in true democracy in Tunisia. It was a bit frightening to see such dramatic results from our efforts. While still not convinced, as were some Anons (like Barrett Brown) that information could topple dictatorships - it clearly could piss off large numbers of people. It was the first time that I, as a hacktivist - had worked a 12 hour shift and then saw with my own eyes such a dramatic result from that effort. But it would not be the last time. In fact, I didn't know it then but such moments were about to come with a quite alarming frequency.

As dawn broke in Tunisia and masses of people took to the streets, the focus in the Op Tunisia channel shifted to a more offensive footing as a series of DdoS attacks upon various Tunisian government web sites was launched.

The targets were soft and toppled easily, and the Tunisian reporters who had found their way (I strongly suspect with the assistance of one Barrett Brown) into the IRC created a sort of instant feed-back loop to the Tunisian protesters regarding the take downs. Tunisians were incredibly encouraged by these take-downs, seeing for the first time someone able to reach out and give, however symbolically - the Bin Ali regime a bloody nose.

Wednesday - January 5, 2011 approx. 9:00 AM PT - Coffee To The People Cafe - San Francisco, California USA

The past 48 hours had been a complete blur. Working furiously for 15 hour stretches in the IRC channels, catching a few hours sleep in Golden Gate Park. Occasionally I would pause and look up from the computer screen and take in all the patrons of the coffee house, and the barristas waiting on them. How would I explain to them that I am calmly sitting there in the virtual company of thousands from around the world, waging an un-seeable cyber war against an intransigent mid-eastern dictatorship. And winning. We were winning! The wildest fantasies of the cyber-punk fiction writers of the late 80's and early 90's was coming true before my eyes. In fact, I was one small part of creating this new reality. Like everything related to Anonymous lately, it was surreal in the extreme. How could a bunch of geeks, hackers and activists spread out in coffee houses, libraries - and student digs around the world be wielding geo-political power?

But the fact was, it did appear as if the Bin Ali regime was weakening. They were certainly getting desperate. My own "crew" in the PLF were performing admirably, and we were slowly growing in number. Not only had we gained some members online, but we had one new physical recruit. A gentleman in his mid-fifties whom I shall call "Frank".

Frank had extensive special forces military training and a severely anti-government attitude. He had appointed himself as my personal security, and was taking his responsibility quite seriously. I did feel safer, especially with my head so buried in my computer that the FBI could just walk right up on me without Frank's ever watchful eyes. As I logged in that morning and started to scroll the news and twitter feeds, the first fire of the day erupted in the IRC. Apparently the Tunisian hackers had discovered that the Tunisian government was using the national routers and malicious code to "phish" people's Facebook and Twitter login data within Tunisia. The problem was dire, but the solution came fast. Within the hour, hackers in Anonymous had remotely connected to one of the computers belonging to a hacker in Tunisia and obtained the malicious code being injected by the Tunisian security forces. The script was not complex, and within two hours of capturing the code - a browser plugin had been created that could easily thwart the malicious code.

The rest of the day was spent spamming the plugin into Tunisia via any method we could think of. It was at this point that it began to slowly dawn on us that we would need to be more proactive in monitoring the Tunisian cyber space. Working groups began to form ad-hoc side-channels to do tasks such as monitor connectivity, censorship - and attempts by the regime to launch cyber attacks on activists or journalists. Other channels formed dedicated to Anons working with Tunisian activists and media people one on one to help them learn encryption and other tools that could keep them safe and amplify their message. We had no way of knowing it at the time, but we were forming a template of an entire new genre of Anonymous Operations.

With Op Chanology and Payback we had seen the cementing of the Censorship Ops, now we were participating in the birth of what would quickly become known as the *Freedom Operations*. But the situation was so intense there was no time to contemplate the historic significance of our actions.

We were a global collective of hackers and activists simply doing our best to topple a dictator who was clearly on the ropes.

Friday - January 7, 2011 approx. 9:30 AM PT - Coffee To The People Cafe - San Francisco, California USA

My trust and friendship with many hard-core Anons was growing every day. And one Anon that I was growing increasing close too was Barrett Brown. It was an honor, Barrett was a consummate activist and a huge part of this idea called Anonymous. He pinged me in PM within seconds of logging in to IRC.

Barrett Brown: Hey X...

X: Good morning. What can I do for you?

Barrett Brown: I have some Tunisian hackers here I want you to talk to. Help them if you can, I think this might be important.

X: Will do, send them to me.

I waited a few minutes and passed the time scrolling back through the feeds to see what I had missed while I briefly caught some shut-eye. After about 15 minutes I got a ping on PM.

Anonymous Tunisia: Hello...

X: Greetings friend, how can I help you today?

Anonymous Tunisia: We are Anons in Tunisia. We have infiltrated the networks of our central bank and the Interior Ministry.

We have found documents proving that there is huge corruption within the security forces in our country. We need help extracting the documents from the servers and publishing them.

Wow. Now that is a message you don't receive everyday. I flipped up the tab with Barrett's PM channel and typed...

X: Hey, do you have anyway to reach Julian?

There was a long pause then Barrett wrote back...

Barrett Brown: Yes.

X: The Tunisians have access to some pretty strong stuff, documents - I think WikiLeaks would be best able to deal with them. They need my help grabbing the data, but based on what I have seen of the government networks in Tunisia that shouldn't be a problem.

Barrett Brown: Will you help them?

X: Yes, if we can we'll do it. I'll keep you apprised.

I flipped back to the tab with the Tunisians and wrote...

X: Send me the data you have on the networks.

After a wait that seemed forever but was probably less than an hour, I finished downloading a zipped file from the Tunisian Anons. Inside were screen shots and notes written in broken English on the two infiltrated networks. One was the central bank of Tunisia, the other appeared to be the primary server for the Ministry of Interior. A small handful of the documents had already been captured and cross-referenced and the material was pure dynamite -

documenting direct bribe payments to security officials in a virtually forensic manner. I quickly gathered my own crew as well as a couple of AntiSec folks and we created a private back-channel in IRC and set to work. The Tunisian government security was so poor that it actually took much longer to download the stolen data than it did to kick in the back doors and enter the networks. The material was explosive, and it needed much more media savvy than we had at that time to get this information out. A member of our group was tasked with going to the WikiLeaks IRC server and making contact while the rest of the team continued the analysis and cross referencing. It took a few hours, but after finally receiving a promise to do their best - the entire data set including our analysis was zipped up and delivered to WikiLeaks.

Monday - January 10, 2011 approx. 10:30 AM PT - Coffee To The People Cafe - San Francisco, California USA

Chaos reigned across Tunisia. Hundreds of thousands had taken the streets. The leaks published by WikiLeaks had helped to fuel the outrage, and the hacking of virtually the entire Tunisian government cyber space had encouraged the protesters. And in large part due to Anonymous actions, the main stream media in the west was finally starting to cover the story. The downside was the regime was feeling the heat, and beginning to panic. Plain clothes security forces were starting to simply shoot and kill protesters on a frighteningly regular basis. Snipers were being deployed, and the death and injury toll was mounting rapidly.

With most of the Tunisian government offline, and a huge trove of leaked information published - our focus turned to one of support for activists and journalists in Tunisia. Media and protesters would join the IRC, voice their particular needs or issues -

and Anons would then craft individual solutions for them. This could take the form of anything from teaching them how to use TOR to building an entire website for them. Separately, another contingent of Anons worked on monitoring the Tunisian cyber space and doing chores like validating the SSL certificates of websites to help Tunisians avoid man-in-the-middle hack attacks. But while this aspect of Operation Tunisia got almost no media attention, and is rarely mentioned in historical accounts of Anonymous involvement in the Jasmine Revolution - it represented by far the largest expenditure of raw manpower in the Op. This focus was also historic, the first ever global crowd sourced tech support for a peaceful revolution. And no street revolution after Tunisia would ever be the same for it. And we could feel it, as it was happening. There was this electric sense during the frantic activities of those days that we were making history in so many ways. And for the first time, we began to see protesters wearing the iconic Guy Fawkes mask and directly associating themselves with Anonymous. It was breathtaking to participate in.

Although we didn't know it at the time, we were halfway through the now famous "Jasmine Revolution". And despite the anarchistic nature of Anonymous, things were working remarkably smoothly. From all over the world, thousands of Anons had come together in the IRC channels with hundreds of Tunisian activists. And everything technically possible was being done to support those activists and to thwart the Bin Ali regime. The hacktivists and the freedom fighters of the Mideast had joined forces, and we were bringing down a dictator in real-time.

Saturday - January 15, 2011 approx. 12:30 PM PT - Coffee To The People Cafe - San Francisco, California USA

When the end came it caught us all, Anon and Tunisian alike – by complete surprise.

One moment the protests raged in the streets and the bullets were flying and Anons were online furiously working against the regime, and the next there was silence in the IRC as the news was announced that Bin Ali had fled the country for refuge in Saudi Arabia. As a final gift to the Tunisian people, Anonymous tracked and helped to apprehend several of Bin Ali's family who escaped to Montreal, Canada with a whole lot of gold belonging to the Tunisian people. And Anonymous Tunisia, only the third National Cell in Anonymous (there are now over 100) was born. Anonymous was morphing from a movement of mostly western hackers in the USA and UK into a truly Global Collective of resistance. And that momentous change began in that IRC during those ten amazing days of the Jasmine Revolution. The Freedom Operations had begun.

The next ten days saw many of us Anons frantically trying to analyze and improve our response in Tunisia as reports began to pour in of protests cropping up across the mid-east. The Anonymous Care Package we had used in Tunisia was revamped. Many hours were spent brainstorming various tactics the Tunisian regime had used to thwart the protesters online, and how to improve our own strategies for combating them. I consulted with Barrett Brown to find out his thoughts on what would happen next. He answered me with just one word: "Egypt...."

Tuesday - January 25, 2011 approx. 10:00 AM PT - Coffee To The People Cafe - San Francisco, California USA

Almost exactly ten days after the end of the Jasmine Revolution in Tunisia, Anonymous entered the fray in the Egyptian protests. I had some hard debates with Barrett Brown and others over the viability of trying to topple the dictator Mubarak. He was even beloved by former Israeli Prime Ministers, and he had signed the Camp David Peace Accords with Israel.

But Barrett was adamant, with our help the people of Egypt could topple this long ruling tyrant. I didn't believe we could, but I did believe in Barrett Brown. So I kept my reservations to myself, and into Tahir Square we sailed the Armada called Anonymous.

The Mubarak regime threw down the gauntlet at Anonymous' feet almost immediately by blocking what had become one of the main media and organizing tools of these protests – Twitter. Our response was immediate, and developed organically from the fact that we already had several dozen Tahir Square protesters in the IRC channel #OpEgypt. Anons within minutes of the Twitter cut-off began taking reports from the ground and tweeting them out on their own or Anonymous affiliated accounts. Everyone pitched in by re-tweeting these posts. Within an hour certain key activists in Egypt had even turned over administrative control of their Twitter accounts to trusted Anons, who would then cut and paste the activists posts from IRC and Tweet them out. This turn of events made the Mubarak regime furious, that they could not silence these protesters - and unbeknownst to us at the time, the regime began plotting a much more sinister way to thwart the flow of information out of and into Tahir Square.

During the early stages of the Egyptian Revolution I worked in two principle areas, media and offensive cyber-attacks. I worked with Barrett Brown to write the Anonymous press release announcing Anonymous Operation Egypt (a follow-up Anonymous PR was written entirely by myself), and for the first time I began helping give the interviews for an insatiable press corp. But by far the more gratifying task was in working with a great team of dedicated Anons to devastate the Egyptian government online infrastructure with brutal and long-lasting attacks that within days left the Mubarak regime a smoking crater in cyber-space. Virtually every Egyptian government website was effected by these rolling attacks which primarily took the form of a combination of DdoS attacks and defacements.

Another area where my work had an impact was in data collection. Instead of using a large number of volunteers to painstakingly harvest the incredibly valuable fax numbers and E-Mail addresses in Egypt, as we had in Tunisia – I programmed a "spider". A spider is a software program designed to crawl servers and harvest specific data. Mine was programmed to collect the fax numbers and E-Mail addresses of every single Egyptian. My spider, which I nick-named "Hazel" - was not only capable of doing the task - but she could then separate the civilian from the government data. This would eventually allow Anonymous to wage psychological warfare on the Egyptian government while at the same time sending valuable information and encouragement to the Egyptian people. And thanks to "Hazel" (who remains an invaluable part of my cyber-arsenal), we accomplished it with far less labor than it took in Tunisia.

Hazel had just one draw back. She could not be turned off during a crawl or she would have to start over. This led to a somewhat comical scene of me having to spend the night sleeping in an alley behind the coffee house so I could stay connected and keep Hazel running. Ironically, it was the most sleep I got during the entire Egyptian Revolution!

Thursday - January 27, 2011 approx. 10:30 PM PT – Cafe Mediterraneum - Berkeley, California USA

A day that will live in infamy within the history of Anonymous, and the world. A ruthless dictator was about to do something that we in Anonymous doubted was even possible. And then it happened. Mubarak turned *off* the Internet in Egypt. For the *entire* country. And the way he did it was particularly brutal. Having tried twice in the past 48 hours to turn off the national connectivity at the ISP/national router level, and having been rebuffed by ITs in Egypt and Anonymous hackers –

he dynamited the only fiber-optic cable running into Egypt at the point where it exits the Mediterranean. Essentially the dictator pulled the plug out of the wall, and for the first time in modern history a nation went dark.

I remember the moment like it was yesterday, and the abject terror that gripped me and the other Anons as all the Egyptians in our IRC disappeared within seconds. Egypt had gone dark, and Anonymous knows well what governments do in the dark places. I and others openly wondered in those first few minutes after the cut-off if the Mubarak regime was about to pull a "Tienanmen Square" by mowing down all the protesters in Tahir Square. The thought was utterly terrifying.

As the shock wore off, and the news of the historic cut-off spread around the world – I retired to a back channel in IRC that was brainstorming ways to get around even this seemingly irrevocable severing of a nation's connectivity to the Internet. Over the course of the next several hours a package of solutions was painstakingly assembled. Utilizing everything from 500 donated dial-up lines, satellite phones with meshnets, and even an obscure way to send packets over ham radio was put together into a single PDF document and faxed to every civilian fax machine in Egypt. And by late evening extremely grateful Egyptians were slowly returning to Twitter and the IRC channel. To my utter amazement, and that of the world – Anonymous had thwarted a dictator in his ultimate bid to isolate his nation. The lights were back on in Tahir Square. And it took less than twelve hours.

And the Egyptians were really pissed off. What had until then been reasonably peaceful protests (with the exception of the brutality of the Egyptian police), quickly morphed into huge full scale riots. This is the ultimate irony of the Mubarak Internet shut-off, he did it to calm the protests down and it had the opposite effect of inflaming them further. It was not the last mistake Mubarak would make in his final week in power, but it was the most devastating to his regime.

And in a strange turn of events, the order to cut the fiber optic line into Egypt was the first of the many charges Mubarak was found guilty of when he was eventually tried in Egyptian court. He received a five year sentence for this particular crime against his people.

Friday - February 11, 2011 approx. 11:00 PM PT – Starbucks Mountain View, California USA

"President Hosni Mubarak has resigned" with those words the Vice President of Egypt set off a massive and epic celebration in Tahir Square. Like waves, that celebration of freedom would reverberate around the world within minutes and even in the streets of Mountain View, California the people were ecstatic and glued to television broadcasts of the festivities in Cairo.

Many westerners were especially blown away. For most of them it was the first time they had ever seen people rise up peacefully and take down their own government. It was a cathartic moment those in the USA would recall later when Occupy Wall Street began its rise. Governments across the globe were beginning to fear their people, rather than the other way around.

This was a pivotal moment for Anonymous as well. It's one thing to punch governments around the world in the nose over this issue or that, but the thought that information activism could play such a vital role in actually toppling these governments was mind-bending to us.

The "Arab Spring" (a term that only appeared after Egypt) was changing the world, and Anonymous. Thousands of people in the mid-east began to identify as Anons. And in addition to Anonymous Tunisia, Anonymous Egypt, Anonymous Iran, Anonymous Libya, and Anonymous Syria made their appearance in quick succession. We were quickly morphing into a true Global Collective.

The original Freedom Operations continued after Egypt with Operation Libya (successful), Operation Iran (a failure) and Operation Syria (an abject failure). It would spawn a series of African Freedom Operations, and inform all future protest support Ops. Eventually, Freedom Operations would stand out as a second genre of Ops after Censorship Operations. The Freedom Operations created a template for how cyber-activists could successfully support and influence ground based protesters. The impact of that moment of innovation by Anonymous continues to be truly epic and historic.

On a personal level, they were exhausting. I participated in every single Op mentioned, and as robustly as I did in those I have recounted here. For at least a month the sleep I got was often a few hours every few days. And through out I was of course being hounded and man-hunted around the Bay Area of northern California by the FBI, who often were only days behind me. I moved constantly from coffee house to coffee house, city to city – more or less in a big circle around the Bay Area. Also after this series of Ops, Barrett Brown took his formal leave of Anonymous and passed his media baton to me. Thanks to his incredible tutoring, I was now writing press releases and giving media interviews like a boss.

The USA had taken note of our rise, and our wielding of geo-political power – and they were not impressed. In fact, the government of the USA was (and continues to be) terrified of us. And they were about to unleash upon Anonymous a plan so diabolical it's like has not been seen for hundreds of years. Still extremely pissed off about our alignment with WikiLeaks, the government of the USA was about to declare open war on Anonymous. People would fall, but Anonymous would rise triumphant.

Author's Note: The roughly two week period from January 27th to February 11th in 2011 remains as one of the most intense periods for me personally in Anonymous.

And it stands as the most prominent pivotal moment for Anonymous historically. During this brief period, as I began to gain my stride in my run from the FBI, we saw two dictators fall, the birth of the "Arab Spring", the advent of the Anonymous Freedom Operations, the number of participants involved in Anonymous grow a hundred-fold, and the birth of the first "National Cells" within Anonymous. And as the next two chapters will explore, during this *same* two week period we also saw Anonymous take down a federal security contractor, destroy its CEO's life, and be hit by the FBI in one of the largest coordinated raids in law enforcement history.

Suffice it to say that it was breath-taking, and few of the Anons I knew (including myself) got a heck of a lot of sleep those two weeks. It's hard to describe just how much Anonymous grew in power and scope, and how much of its future mythology – was forged during the crucible of those two weeks in 2011. It was becoming clear to me that I was caught up in a rip-tide of history, and all I could do was stand and deliver. My fate had become inexorably intertwined with that of Anonymous.

This Chapter, and the following two Chapters – deal with separate strands of this story that wound their way through this same general two week time period. I could think of no other way to properly highlight the importance of these events without separating them into different chapters. But it is important to keep in mind while reading that all of these events actually happened simultaneously. But as confusing as this all may be to the reader, it's worth the extra hassle. Because everything, *absolutely everything* – that happened after that epic time period in 2011, was caused directly by the events of those two weeks.

FIVE

The FBI Raids

"You can not arrest an idea." ~~ Topiary

Thursday - January 27, 2011 approx. 10:00 AM PT – Caffe Mediterraneum - Berkeley, California USA

Do you know why Friday the 13th is considered an extremely unlucky day? Most people don't. On Friday – October 13, 1307 at the exact same hour the combined forces of King Philip IV of France and the Pope spread out across Europe and the Middle-East and raided all known headquarters of the Knights Templar and arrested nearly every member of the organization. Regardless of what you think about the Templars, it was and is a brutal tactic to use against any group of people. And on this day, as Anonymous successfully battled Mubarak to keep the Internet turned on in Egypt - the FBI launched just such an attack on Anonymous USA. In a disturbing sign of coordination, there were simultaneous raids by Scotland Yard in the UK as well. And it was nothing short of a resounding declaration of war against Anonymous....

One of the many benefits of being immersed in the realm of information activism is that you pretty much get any relevant breaking news in real time. It's sort of like sitting in the front seat of humanity with your nose against the windshield of history. Shit comes at you fast. The news broke early in the morning, on the worst possible day for it in the history of Anonymous. As we scrambled desperately to thwart the dictator Mubarak and keep the Internet turned on in Egypt, it was on Twitter that the first reports appeared. An army of FBI agents had fanned out across the USA from coast to coast, and had kicked in the doors of dozens of Anons while serving over 40 search warrants. All computers and electronics were seized, even those belonging to family members or room-mates. Even game consoles were taken. Folks of all ages from a grandmother to a teenage girl were dragged from their homes before dawn and arrested.

But there was one Anon on their list they didn't capture that day. *Me.* When I caught the news I was in San Francisco. The moment my self-appointed body guard Frank heard about the raids, he practically dragged me to his van and insisted on relocating me to Berkeley immediately. The rest of that day was a blur, as I sat in the cafe for twelve hours working with other hackers from around the globe trying desperately to keep Egypt connected to the Internet. But the news reports on the raids were everywhere in everyone's feeds - and the mood within Anonymous was somber....and angry. But due to the frenzied activity surrounding the Egyptian Revolution and our involvement in it, it would be almost two weeks before some of us could come together with a plan. That plan would have a name, one that gained total consensus fast. *Anonymous Operation Vendetta.* "Op V" was the shorthand code name.

As the details began to trickle in on Twitter it became painfully obvious the FBI had chosen their targets carefully. Many good and influential Anons, whom I had worked with this past few weeks - had their doors kicked in. The_N0, Trivette, and even our own Absolem - all had been attacked at dawn for the crime of being Anonymous, their doors dropped and all their electronics taken. No doubt I also would have been targeted during this sweep, except I had already anticipated the possibility and escaped the dragnet. But the intel I was getting from the streets in the Bay Area was that the feds were literally everywhere looking for me. Only the fact that I kept moving and kept to the shadows of society helped me escape capture by the FBI Cyber Crime Division.

Saturday - February 5, 2011 approx. 2:00 PM PT - Starbucks Mountain View, California USA

A few of the veterans from the ongoing "Arab Spring" Freedom Ops had taken a break and were meeting in a private invite only IRC channel to discuss the apparent declaration of war by the USDOJ and GCHQ. Barrett Brown, Greg Housh - and a few others I can't recall were present. It was decided that the Op would be called Operation Vendetta, or "Op V" for short. After hours of discussion, a three pronged approach was agreed upon. There would be a public face to Operation Vendetta, the usual smashy smashy on the USA and UK government servers - in tandem with a Press Release and video.

But something new also developed, the idea of secret projects that were not public knowledge. In that vein, two additional covert components to Op V were discussed. It was agreed that Barrett Brown was best equipped to use his contacts to form an ad hoc pro bono legal team of crack lawyers in the USA who would defend our Anons. Barrett was excited by this chore, and already had a couple in mind to reach out to. The second covert aspect of Operation Vendetta was the idea of an "Anonymous Underground Railroad" of safe houses and transportation designed to facilitate any Anons who did not wish to remain under oppression in the USA to escape to Canada. The creation of this ambitious project fell to me.

All of us set to work that very day with great urgency. It was obvious that the USA and UK were serious about this war on Anonymous, and Operation Vendetta was our line of defense - and our line in the sand. As for myself, I set to work contacting people I knew with houses and cars who might be willing to provide protection and sanctuary to fleeing Anons should any choose that route. And I waited for Absolem to make contact. It had been many years since anyone I considered to be in my crew was arrested, and I was extremely uneasy at the fate of one of my youngest and most promising recruits.

Thursday - February 10, 2011 approx. 1:00 PM PT – McDonalds Mountain View, California USA

I had been waiting for days to hear from Absolem. I was dreading what he might tell me. Finally he made an appearance in the IRC and he pinged me in DM almost immediately.

Absolem: Hey X...

Commander X: How are you? Are you ok? Man, I've been worried sick since I saw the news.

Absolem: Yep, it was pretty bad. They broke my door down and put a gun to my head, took everything - even my game console? They questioned me for hours but I told them nothing. They did show me a picture they said was you though. I don't know if it is, but that's what they said.

Commander X: It's ok, just stay calm. We'll get through this, together. You are not alone.

Absolem: Here's the thing though. They found drugs in my apartment. They are threatening to charge my live-in girlfriend with possession if I don't become a confidential informant. They want me to help them capture you.

While I shouldn't have been surprised at this, the revelation still took my breath away. But at least Absolem was coming clean and telling me. I spent several minutes thinking dark thoughts while Absolem waited patiently in the chan. I flipped open a tab and DMed Barrett Brown and asked him if he had managed to nail down any attorneys. He said he had two, but one had been taken already to defend The_N0, aka Mercedes Haefer. I claimed dibs on the other one for Absolem and got the contact details from Barrett.

Absolem: What should I do X?

Commander X: Are you prepared to do what I tell you, Are you still a part of my crew?

Absolem: Yes.

Commander X: Good. Stop talking to the FBI. Tell them to fuck off. I doubt they will actually screw with your girlfriend over this. And contact this attorney now, today.

I gave Asolem the contact info Barrett had given me to one Tom Nolan Attorney At Law, and told him to stay in contact only if he safely could. I flipped open the DM tab for Barrett Brown and asked him to contact this Tom Nolan at once and tell him to expect a call from me soon.

    I sat there staring at my computer screen for a long time, maybe an hour. My thoughts were dark and paranoid. This whole thing seemed to have gone out of control somehow. And now other people were reliant upon me for leadership and guidance in ways that I never would have imagined possible. Somehow I had not only got myself into one hell of a piece of trouble, but others in that same boat were relying on me in part for answers on what to do about it. How had these responsibilities become so grave, so quickly? Was I really prepared to join with a small band of activists and actually wage a cyber war against the USA and the UK? I mean, fuck....Tunisia is one thing, Bin Ali was a god damned douche bag tin-pot dictator. But were we really going to take on the West as well? *REALLY?*

    For the first time I became aware of a strange....*constriction* in my life. It seemed that my options, what was possible - was narrowing to a single set of cascading historical events. And I felt bound to this historical chain reaction in a binary way. It seemed I had but two choices: to continue to surf this strange geo-political karmic wave, or to bail on the whole movie and disappear forever. It was as if fate was zooming in on me, and I almost didn't have a choice in much of anything beyond what to have for dinner. Because quitting just wasn't an option, I am simply too stubborn for that. I said a silent prayer to no god that I would find the inner strength to see this through, no matter what peril or adventure it led me into next. Then I ordered another coffee and set to creating a plan for our Absolem.

First I wrote a PLF Communique and blasted it on Twitter and to the list of journalist E-Mail addresses Barrett Brown had left me with when he stopped doing active PR for Anonymous a few weeks before.

For Immediate Release - PLF Communique

Recently, during the latest wave of arrests here in the USA of Anonymous participants - one of the Commanders of the Peoples Liberation Front was raided. In the process of serving their bogus search warrant, the FBI confiscated Commander Absolem's computer. In addition, the FBI alleges to have found some drugs on the premises, which they are threatening to charge a lady acquaintance with if Commander Absolem refuses to "cooperate" with their "investigation" of Anonymous and the PLF.

The Peoples Liberation Front condemns in the strongest way these tactics of extortion and intimidation. It boggles the mind that the PLF and Anonymous would spend weeks defending the Egyptians from just such tactics on the part of their police against peaceful activists, only to be faced with the very same here in the supposedly "free" USA. The PLF and Anonymous have a legal team, and they are working hard at this very moment to defend Commander Absolem and the other Anonymous participants who have chosen to stand and fight these ridiculous charges. This is nothing more than the same old crap the FBI has been doing for 60 years, from the Communist witch hunts of the 50s, to the CoinTelPro investigations - to the ongoing harassment of political activists across the country recently reported in the media.

The Peoples Liberation Front has a message for the FBI. We are NOT afraid of you. You will NOT be subverting our members, and you especially will get nothing further from Commander Absolem. You should take a hard look at the Interior Ministry police of Egypt and realize that you are no different; you are jack booted thugs. And the PLF will deal with you as they do all the enemies of freedom around the world. And that begins now with this Press Release sent to every media outlet in the world.

We are NOT Egyptians. This is NOT Tunisia. In the USA robust free speech is not only a basic right, it is our culture and history. The Peoples Liberation Front (and we suspect Anonymous will concur) won't stand idly by while the FBI spends taxpayer dollars to attempt to subvert and shut down legal political activism. If we need to put millions of people in the streets of DC then so be it, we will not shrink from a "Red, White & Blue Revolution" to follow up the "Jasmine Revolution" and the "Lotus Revolution" of Tunisia and Egypt.

To the world, to all who support freedom and especially to those who believe in the aims of the Peoples Liberation Front and Anonymous: Now is the time to stand and fight with us to defend ourselves against the same tyranny we have so often defended others against. Remember, YOU are Anonymous !

As is so often the case when I do Anonymous PR work, the interview requests came in almost immediately. I gave a handful of them that afternoon, emphasizing that Anonymous was prepared in every way to defend its own and engage this war. The media was still buzzing over the Anonymous Operation Vendetta Press Release and video that had come out the day before.

The USDOJ had thrown down the gauntlet at Anonymous' feet, and now we had responded with our best. The Global Cyber War well and truly began on this day, when the empire of the USA came to stand toe to toe with the most powerful collective of hacktivists in world history.

I then took out my burner cell phone, and stepped outside to have a smoke and call this new Attorney that Barrett Brown had scored for us. His secretary answered on the second ring, and asked who was calling. I told her I thought "Commander X" was a bit pretentious, so just tell him it's "Mr. X" on the line. She failed to see the humor in this, but she connected the call anyway when I told her Mr. Nolan was expecting me to ring.

Tom Nolan: Hello?

Commander X: Greetings Mr. Nolan. My name is X. I believe you are expecting my call?

Tom Nolan: Normally I don't talk to people who won't tell me their name.

Commander X: *chuckle* Well, then I do appreciate you making an exception for me. But who I am is not important Mr. Nolan. As I understand it you have volunteered to represent an Anon pro bono. We have a case for you, one of the "PayPal 14". I believe you already have his details via fax from Barrett?

Tom Nolan: Yes, I have them here. Ok, I'll represent him. Is there anything else....*Mr. X*?

Commander X: There is, in fact. This young man is very important to me, Mr. Nolan. I want you to represent him as if he were your own child.

Tom Nolan: I represent all my clients equally, and to the best of my ability.

Commander X: *Like your own child*, Mr. Nolan. *Don't* let us down.

    I snapped off the phone before a flustered and clearly angry Mr. Nolan could respond to my veiled threat. I turned the cheap burner phone off and removed the battery, which I hurled into the bushes beside the McDonalds. I then dropped the phone to the sidewalk, stepped on it hard and kicked the pieces into the storm drain.
    It should be noted for the record that it was Absolem during Anonymous Operation Egypt who worked with Egyptian activists and set up the very first live streams of the Arab Spring. How ironic that an incredibley talented, brilliant, and honorable cyber freedom fighter like Absolem, who only days before had played a pivotal role in the Egyptian Revolution - would now face the same persecution for protesting that those Egyptians faced....*in the USA*. So many heroes were being created during this early frantic and formative period of Anonymous history. People were already paying a price with their liberty. And a few would eventually pay with their lives even.

Wednesday - June 29, 2011 approx. 10:30 PM PT – Cafe Mediterraneum - Berkeley, California USA

A series of additional FBI raids and arrests of those suspected to be involved with Anonymous had taken place about two weeks prior, and Operation Vendetta was receiving a renewed attention. The tweet scrolled down my time line after yet another mind-numbingly long day of work on these Anonymous projects. It was from the account of what appeared to be a criminal Attorney in southern California, Ventura to be exact.

He was praising Anonymous, expressing sympathy for the latest round of FBI raids - and offering to represent any Anons arrested pro-bono. On a lark, and mostly because I was exhausted - I tweeted back: "Mr. Leiderman does that include the infamous Commander X?". Less than a minute past before he replied: "That especially includes the infamous Commander X!".

Interesting. Ok lawyer dude, we can play a bit. I looked up his website and fired off a quick E-Mail to this Jay Leiderman.

Greetings Mr. Leiderman --

I am the infamous hacktivist known as "Commander X" who tweeted about your offer to help Anons with representation.

First, I don't want history to show you worked for me pro bono, I'll pay you a symbolic dollar - more when I get it. Second, no way you can be my attorney unless I meet you in person. I will reveal my identity and give you my legal files at that time.

YOURS -- X

A few hours later I received his reply.

X --

Agreed. How do we proceed?

-- Jay

Monday - July 4, 2011 approx. 10:30 AM PT – Cafe Mediterraneum Berkeley, California USA

After my initial exchange with Jay Leiderman I met with one of my comrades in Berkeley. "Zero" was a PLF and Anonymous supporter, and a local radical activist. I had revealed my true identity to him weeks before, and he was ever willing to help. Together we spent hours brainstorming a protocol for someone physically meeting with me. It took awhile, but we finally came up with a plan and sent the instructions to Jay Leiderman. And now it was crunch time - the day of the meeting had arrived.

The plan now was to have Jay stroll around downtown Berkeley, following a path being live texted to him by me - and secretly tailed and watched closely by Zero. Zero in turn would text me with how Jay was doing, and his observations - and I would then text Jay with the next way point. "He's smiling, I think he's actually enjoying this", Zero texted me at one point. We did this until Jay was positively sweating from the July heat of the Bay Area. Finally I led him back to where I was sitting quietly on my backpack in front of the coffee house, patiently thumbing away on my phone. I was sitting on the ground under a shade tree on University Avenue next to an elderly white haired old man with a long pony tail who regularly set up a table there selling political stickers. I knew he had several involving WikiLeaks and Bradley Manning, so I thought I would have one last bit of fun with the man who I had affectionately dubbed "The Lawyer Dude".

As Jay rounded the corner into sight and paused for my next text, I sent "See the man selling stickers? Approach him and maybe buy a couple". Jay looked up and saw the man next to me and smiled, he obviously thought that *he* was the infamous "Commander X" he had come to meet. He bounded up to the table, just feet away from me. I had to tip my hat down over my face to keep Jay from seeing me giggle hysterically as he proudly bought a few stickers and then stood there just grinning at the poor old man who was completely perplexed by him. I surreptitiously sent Jay one last text message:

"See the man sitting NEXT to the guy selling stickers? Wrap your business card in a $20.00 bill and give it to him, go to People's Park around the corner - and sit down anywhere".

I slung on my backpack and followed behind Jay a few hundred feet while he rounded the corner and found an empty bench in the iconic People's Park of Berkeley. How ironic that I would meet this man here, where so much blood was spilled just to liberate one small park from the clutches of a greedy University in the 60's. In many ways this park was the epicenter and starting point of modern resistance in America.

A slightly confused and very sweaty Jay Leiderman looked up at me as I shrugged off the pack and sat down, "X, I presume?". "You presume correctly Lawyer Dude, welcome to the revolution" I replied as I shook his hand. Jay Leiderman reminds me of Buddha. He has a cherubic face and near perpetual smile. While he is Greek in background, he actually looks sort of Irish, with curly locks and youthful features. Jay was smart, gentile, humorous - and most importantly enthusiastic in his support of Anonymous. I liked him right away.

Over the next few hours we sat there in People's Park as I told him my story, how I had come to be on the run from an FBI manhunt. I gave him my ID and legal paperwork. And we talked about Anonymous, and the breath-taking events unfolding around us. "Sometimes Jay I feel like we've been granted the power of God, and it scares the fuck out of me" I told him as the sun began to set in the west. Jay and I took a cab to the train station to see him off to the airport.

Standing on the platform, Jay asked me if there was anything else he could do. "Well Lawyer Dude, you got any money on you?" I asked. Jay pulled out his wallet, there was a decent stack of bills inside. "How much do you need to get to the airport?" I asked. He pulled out a twenty dollar bill and said, "this should cover it". "Good" I said as I reached inside his wallet and took all the rest of his money.

Without blinking I turned and started to walk down the platform. "Hey, wait!" Jay yelled after me. I froze, and then slowly turned around. "You never told me if I'm hired" he said. I smiled and strolled back to face him. Pulling out the wad of bills I had just fished out of his wallet, I thumbed through until I found a single dollar bill - which I then handed to Jay. "Yes" I said over my shoulder as I turned and walked away.

SIX

The HB Gary Affair

"Faster than you can say: 'get these hornets off my penis' - Anonymous took down Barr's website, stole his E-Mails, deleted the company's back-up data, trashed his Twitter account - and remotely wiped his iPad."
~~ Stephen Colbert

Saturday - February 5, 2011 approx. 7:00 PM PT – McDonalds - Mountain View, California USA

All day, things had been hot and heavy in Operation Egypt. We didn't know it at that time but we were only about five days away from Mubarak stepping down, and another resounding and historic victory for Anonymous. The work flow was becoming a bit confused, also. I had been drafted into a parallel Anonymous Operation Iran by a hacktivist who went by "TarenCapel" and an Iranian ex-patriot called "Arash".

Today I had learned a hard lesson in cyber warfare, namely that there are many players on this chess board. And not all of them were, shall we say - reasonable actors. I had discovered in my research for Op Iran that there was a group of "pro-regime" hackers in Iran called the "Iranian Cyber Army". Brashly, and without consulting either Arash or TarenCapel, I had reached out to these hackers with a long emotional and very eleoquent message asking them to switch sides and join with Anonymous to take down Khomeni. The response from the ICA was as swift as it was brutal. Less than half an hour after sending the message Anonymous and the PLF suffered a devastating multi-pronged cyber attack that all but wiped us both from the Internet. The Anons in all the other Ops, not to mention Op Iran - were really pissed at me and I had to spend hours debriefing on my stupidity with TarenCapel and Arash. My mind was numb, and I was in no position to deal with yet another crisis that day when Barrett Brown pinged me into a DM session.

Barrett Brown: Hey X....how are you?

Commander X: Tired. What can I do for you?

Barrett Brown: Have you seen this?

Barrett sent me a link to a Financial Times article that had come out the day before. In the article, the CEO of cyber security contracter HB Gary Federal, one Aaron Barr - claimed that he had invented a sophisticated system of analysis to un-mask secret groups using publicly available data points like social media. He further claimed that he had demonstrated this new technique by targeting Anonymous over the past several weeks. He had identified dozens of Anons, so he said - including the top five "Generals" and top twenty "Lieutenants". He further boasted that he was going to sell this list to the FBI.

Commander X: Shit....

Barrett Brown: Some of us have gathered in the IRC back channel #InternetFeds to plan a response, you are invited to join us. We're going to get Barr's "list", and do some other things.

Commander X: I'm honored, but with Op Egypt and now Op Iran, I am swamped. But can you have someone keep me posted?

Barrett Brown: Will do. If you change your mind, just ping me.

As I closed the tab and leaned back to stretch, I was thinking that the Anonymous response to a challenge like what Aaron Barr had thrown down would take....some time. Days, maybe weeks I guessed. I was wrong, by a long shot...

Sunday - February 6, 2011 approx. 8:30 PM PT – Starbucks - Mountain View, California USA

Aaron Barr knew he was in trouble long before the kick off on Superbowl Sunday. Sitting in his home and prepared to relax and watch the game, his E-Mails would later show that an earlier series of

DdoS attacks by Anonymous in response to his Financial Times interview the day before had him and his fellows at HB Gary Federal quite concerned initially. But when nothing else happened for several hours they began to get cocky, bragging that Anonymous was a bunch of impotent script-kiddies with no teeth. It was just about kick-off time when the other ball dropped. The DdoS attacks had been mere cover fire for a much more devastating attack that had quietly unfolded during the night. Barr got his first signal that something was amiss when he got a call from an HB Gary Federal employee telling him the company website was *gone*. He asked if they meant DdoSed and they told him no, it was just *gone*. He asked why they didn't replace it with a backup copy, and was informed that they were also *gone*. At that moment, a tingle ran up Aaron Barr's spine as he realized he was in very, very deep shit.

He reached for his iPad to try and Tweet out some official response to the still unfolding hack. As he powered up the pad, the screen went blue on him. It had been remotely wiped. Aaron Barr looked up at a photo of the twin towers on fire after 9/11 that hung on his wall, and reached over to pull the plug on his home router. There would be no Superbowl for Aaron Barr this year. In fact one might surmise that since the day marks his complete downfall, Aaron Barr doesn't quite enjoy Superbowl Sunday the same as he used to before that fateful day.

As Aaron Barr raced across DC to his office to try and get a handle on the attack, the Anons were busy making a complete ass of him on his own Twitter account - which they had also hijacked during the night. It was when Aaron Barr arrived in DC and assessed the true extent of the cyber attack, namely that Anonymous had also taken all HB Gary Federal documents and over seventy thousand internal E-Mails that he became desperate enough to turn to me to try and help him. He pinged me in the Op Iran channel, and we went to DM.

Aaron Barr: X, can we talk?

Commander X: So talk.

Aaron Barr: Anonymous has this all wrong, this was all just a thought experiment. I was trying to show how Anonymous might be vulnerable. I wasn't going to sell anything to the FBI.

Commander X: Whatever. What do you want from me?

Aaron Barr: Can you maybe call off the dogs?

Commander X: Just curious, you do know they have all your docs and E-Mail - right?

Aaron Barr: Can you convince the others not to release that material?

Commander X: Not even if I wanted to, which I most certainly do not. I saw the scans and how vulnerable your servers were. I just hope you saved some of those fat paychecks, they might be stopping soon.

It wasn't long before I got a ping from tFlow.

tFlow: Hey X, did you hear we got Barr's "list" of Anons?

Commander X: I did, from Barrett. Any chance I can get a copy?

tFlow: It's on it way to you now. We'd love to know if Barr got you right. We are trying to asses how accurate this list is and whether to release it, redact it - or what.

Commander X: I'm downloading what you sent me now, give me a few minutes to examine it.

The now infamous "Anonymous List" that Aaron Barr, CEO of HB Gary Federal -

had bragged about to the media, the one that contained the supposed top twenty "lieutenants" and top five "generals" within the Collective - came down as a spread sheet. Screen names and public data were on the left columns, the actual identities were on the right and concealed until you scrolled the document. The minute I opened it I saw that I was number 5 in Aaron Barr's "General" category. How fucking flattering. But had I been correctly identified? I hesitated before I scrolled. I tried to recall all my conversations with Barr prior to our learning who he really was. I had to admit, there was a fair chance he had got me right. How would that affect my run from the FBI? Would I have to leave the West Coast? Bunker in and go underground? This is the first moment in all this I remember thinking I may even have to leave the USA as a dissident. Jesus christ. I scrolled across with my heart pounding....

"Who in the fuck is Ben Devries?" I actually said out loud as I read the identity that Aaron Barr had ascribed to the online persona of "Commander X". Then I read the address Barr alleged for Mr. Devries, and it all fell together what had happened. In an instant, I recalled the conversation weeks ago I had with Barr under his "secret" Anonymous alias before we knew he was a rat. He had reproached me for publicly registering a hacktivist domain name using my real identity, which I had done.

He was right, but I punted and bluffed and told him "you don't actually believe that's my *real* name, do you?". Apparently, Barr had fallen for this and so he looked up the physical address I had registered with - which was random I had just made it up out of thin air. But it turned out to be a real address to a real house. A house in which lived an organic gardener and occasional protester by the name of Ben Devries. Mr. Devries wasn't an Anon, or even a hacker and Ben never even saw the shit storm that hit him coming. I flipped open a tab in IRC and pinged Barrett Brown.

Commander X: You busy?

Barrett Brown: Never to busy for you X. You get a chance to look at Barr's document yet?

Commander X: Yes.

Barrett Brown: Well? Are you Ben Devries? We are trying to gauge how good some of this info of his is. Seems so far about 95% wrong.

Commander X: Well you can add me to the list of those he got wrong. Way wrong. I'm not Ben Devries and I have no clue who that even is.

Barrett Brown: Ok, I'll let them know. Looks like were going to drop the doc online later today. We're even going to send it to the FBI for free just to spite Barr. What are you going to do about this Devries dude?

Commander X: I guess I'll have to make a public statement of some sort when the doc drops, maybe give a few interviews. I can't let some poor innocent guy take the heat for me. This is all so fucked up. I hope Barr chokes on a shrimp cocktail and drops dead. Stupid fucker.

Barrett Brown: Well, if it's any consolation I don't think either Barr or HB Gary will survive this. They've been wrecked pretty bad. I'll send some journos your way that will be happy to talk to you about this.

Commander X: Thanks, my friend.

The mood in Anonymous was positively jubilant. One might even say, triumphal. This douch-bag big-wig security "expert" had directly threatened Anonymous, and the Collective had responded in less than 24 hours. They took his website offline, deleting the back up data, stole seventy thousand E-Mails, and thousands of documents and code, hijacked the CEO's Twitter account, and remotely wiped his iPad at the very moment of the Superbowl Sunday kick-off. The report that Aaron Barr had compiled on Anonymous turned out to be 97% incorrect at identifying Anons, and it was posted to the FBI for free, just to spite HB Gary Federal. Eventually all of the material taken from HB Gary Federal servers was posted to Barrett Brown's latest endeavor, *Project PM*.

Project PM would eventually become Barrett Brown's show piece, and the center of his work. Designed as an open source think tank of sorts, the goal was to analyze the myriad of public information as well as leaks and hacked data in order to map the relationships and money flow in the emerging "Industrial-Surveillance Complex". Like WikiLeaks original concept, it is based on the Wikipedia framework. And the USDOJ now had yet one more reason to paint that bull's eye on Barrett's back just a little bit bigger.

I spent the next two weeks continuing the fight along side TarenCapel and Arash in Operation Iran, and in my spare moments desperately giving as many interviews as I could to clear poor Ben Devries of the accusations that he was....me. Ben's life would never be the same after the *HB Gary Affair*. He would remain bitter and resentful at this insane intrusion into his life for years. I have no idea if he ever sued HB Gary Federal or Aaron Barr, but I certainly hope he somehow managed to get some justice from these criminals in three piece suits.

Aaron Barr would resign in disgrace as CEO of HB Gary Federal. Thanks to a judicious "leak" of some of his stolen data to a particularly sympathetic Senator, hearings on HB Gary Federal were convened in the US Congress. The corpse of HB Gary Federal would eventually be sold off for pennies on the dollar. Aaron Barr would move to New York City, where he eventually found another security firm to give him a job. A job he would promptly get fired from when it was revealed that he had dyed his hair blue, pierced his face -

and was hanging out at OWS in Zuccotti Park trying to infiltrate Anonymous again to exact his revenge on the Collective. At that point his wife left him, taking his children - and his destruction at the hands of Anonymous was complete. And the world through the media had taken note: *do not fuck with Anonymous.*

SEVEN

Creation Of The "Occupy Movement"

"The Occupy Wall Street project feels like a burning ember that might light the torch of justice and inflame our longing for freedom." ~~ James A. Forbes

Sunday - August 14, 2011 approx. 1:00 PM ET - Taco Bell Mountain View, CA - USA

It was an insane spring, and it was shaping up to be a crazier summer. In March I had single handedly launched Anonymous Operation Ivory Coast, a Freedom Op targeting an African dictator. There was a disputed election, protesters on the ground - and a government cyber-space so un-defended that I took it off the Internet with the help of just a couple of hackers in a mere 6 hours. In a matter of weeks, the Dictator and his entire family were in chains and another country had found freedom.

I had travelled to Montana and Idaho in a vain attempt to probe and possibly cross the Canadian border. In a hysterical example of hackers being disconnected from reality, I was turned back by hungry Grizzly bears leaving their dens for Spring. No sooner did I arrive back in the Bay Area with my tail between my legs, then I was to launch my second Anonymous Op on my own.

In March an unarmed homeless man by the name of Thomas Kelly was viciously beaten to death by a Fullerton, California Police Officer who beat his face to a bloody un-recognizable pulp with the butt of his taser, which he burned out zapping Kelly more times than they could count. His father was an ex-cop, and evidence shows that Kelly died praying out-loud for his dad to come help him. Kelly's father was definitely *not* in favor of Anonymous getting involved in the street protests that had engulfed the small city of Fullerton. But his sister, now that was another matter all together. Thomas Kelly's sister looked at things entirely differently. While open to the possibility of getting some sort of justice from the "system", she also understood that the greater measure of justice and social change may come from the streets and online in the form of transgressive protest and disruption. She had reached out to Anonymous through a local hacker.

At the time there were so many Ops going on in the Collective that for a brief period this local hacker's requests for assistance went unanswered. Finally one day he cornered me online while I was still in Berkeley. All he asked was thirty seconds of my time, and he showed me a picture. It was a picture of Thomas Kelly as he lay dying in the trauma unit after his beating at the hands of the Fullerton PD. At first I thought....it was an animal, or some sort of movie prop. It took some puzzling over the image to even realize that it was a *man* I was looking at. The hacker didn't even use up his thirty seconds, he simply said cops did this with their bare hands. Yep, ok - I was in. And so I used what I had learned so far in my own hacktivist career, plus what I had been taught as part of the Freedom Ops - and I launched Anonymous Operation Fullerton on my own from a coffee house on University Avenue. The next day an FBI agent came in with a warrant for the router of the cafe while I was writing the Op Fullerton Press Release. So I moved to Mountain Veiw, where Google had recently announced city-wide free WiFi.

Anonymous Operation Fullerton as it would turn out would be a bit of an innovation in as much as it was the first of a sub-genre that would become known as "FTP" Ops. For those un-enlightened FTP stands for *Fuck The Police*. This sub-genre would reach its maturity years later in another Op I would also launch, *Anonymous Operation Ferguson*. But that's the subject of a whole other book entirely. This also wasn't the first time the FBI had come into a coffee house or other establishment to seize the routers I had been using while I was actually sitting in those places working on Anonymous related things. Twice before, both times in San Francisco - once the two G-men even sat at the table next to me. These guys were literally right on my tail, and I could feel my time running out.

I had tried once half-heartedly to leave the USA. But the fact was that I hesitated for the same reason famous hacker fugitive Kevin Mitnick did. Because once I took that drastic step, I was never coming back home in this lifetime. And that was a decision I was not yet prepared to make.

I had family here, and friends - and many fabulous places I had called home. But it was becoming increasingly clear I would probably be captured, the USA government had very fine-grained control over the matrix within its borders.

In June 2011 I launched yet another Anonymous Op, this time in defense of a very old personal friend of mine. Most people know of the global movement called *Food Not Bombs*. Well, I remember walking through Golden Gate Park in the 80's with the founder Keith McHenry when the entire Food Not Bombs organization was a grocery cart with a five gallon bucket of hot soup in it and a cardboard sign tied on the front that said in black magic marker "Food Not Bombs". We would go set up in Golden Gate Park next to the McDonalds at the end of Haight Street and serve until the cops showed up to stop us, and then run like hell through the park until they caught and arrested us. Yeah, for feeding hungry people - I know.

Now, flash forward three decades, and Orlando, Florida, the entertainment capital of America - decides it would be cool to start violently arresting members of the local chapter of Food Not Bombs for feeding people in a park across from City Hall. That came on my radar almost immediately when I saw it in my news feeds, and I began to closely monitor the situation. When Keith himself flew in to stand with his local chapter and be arrested, I began to prepare *Anonymous Operation Orlando*. They didn't let Keith out of jail for 14 days, but they paid a price as the entire Global Collective of Anonymous cost them many tens of millions in damages from punishing and relentless rolling cyber-attacks. Eventually the City of Orlando went from calling us cyber and *food* terrorists to acceding to all FNB points and even bringing food from the City Hall garden to seal the truce. It took less than three weeks for Anonymous to bring Orlando to its knees. And Food Not Bombs found a shadowy new ally in Anonymous.

Also in June 2011, NATO came out with a report declaring that Anonymous was a serious threat to the national security of member nations, who should coordinate to shut them down. The response from Anonymous was as swift and thorough as it had been with HB Gary Federal. In this case my crew and elements of other crews took the lead. I helped write and distributed the Press Release myself:

Good evening, NATO. We are Anonymous.

It has come to our attention that a NATO draft report has classified Anonymous a potential threat to member states security, and that you seek retaliation against us.

It is true that Anonymous has committed what you would call *cyber-attacks* in protest against several military contractors, companies, lawmakers, and governments, and has continuously sought to fight against threats to our freedoms on the Internet. And since you consider state control of the Internet to be in the best interest of the various nations of your military alliance, you therefore consider us a potential threat to international security.

So we would like to make it clear that we, in reality, pose no threat to the people of your nations. Anonymous is not a reckless swarm attacking the websites of governments and companies out of hatred or spite. We fight for freedom. For ourselves, and the people of the world, we seek to preserve the liberty granted to the millions of people who have found it on the Internet.

In your draft, you mention the data intelligence company HBGary Federal, and how they were hacked by Anonymous. You use this as justification that we are a threat. What you conveniently fail to mention is that HBGary itself was engaged in illegal activity, including but not limited to:

being contracted by the United States Chamber of Commerce to spy on & discredit unions and progressive groups, being contracted by the Bank of America to launch a campaign of misinformation against Wikileaks and its supporters (going so far as to blackmail journalists), developing a new type of Windows rootkit to spy upon individuals, and developing astroturfing software that could make an army of fake social media profiles to manipulate and sway public opinion on controversial issues.

That this company which tries to protect the US Government from hackers was partaking in such illegal activity against ordinary, uninvolved citizens, whether it be for the aid of security or not, is completely disgraceful and utterly unacceptable.

We care not whether the actions we have taken in this struggle have complied with laws of the United States or any other country. What your lot fail to understand is that we live in cyberspace. The only laws that apply are the laws set forth by our individual consciences. We break your nations' laws when we recognize those laws to stand between the people and their freedom.

Anonymous is not simply a group of super hackers. Anonymous is the embodiment of freedom on the web. We exist as a result of the Internet, and humanity itself. This frightens you. It only seems natural that it would. Governments, corporations, and militaries know how to control individuals. It frustrates you that you do not control us. We have moved to a world where our freedom is in our own hands. We owe you nothing for it.

We stand for freedom for every person around the world. You stand in our way.

We hope you come to see that your attempts to censor and control our existence are futile.

But if this is not the case, if you continue to object to our freedoms – we shall not relent.

We do not fear your tyranny. You cannot win a battle against an entity you do not understand. You can take down our networks, arrest every single one of us that you can backtrace, read every bit of data ever shared from computer to computer for the rest of this age, and you will still lose.

So come at me bro. You can retaliate against us in any manner you choose. Lock down the web. Throw us in prison. Take it all away from us. Anonymous will live on.

Within a day we had hacked into the main classified NATO servers and it was basically a free-for-all with everyone in our combined crews simply surfing their database and taking whatever we fancied. Before the NATO IT guys finally managed to detect the hack and lock us out we had ex-filtrated over a Gb of extremely interesting stuff. I personally settled on the NATO Field Manuals for secure communications of deployments. This data set contained all the hardware, software, and set-up instructions for secure encrypted NATO communications - and I found it a fascinating study. I was still downloading it as I gave CBS a text chat interview about the hack. When I told the journalist, he was incredulous - and asked if he could print that. I said sure whatever. The world governments were now truly in awe of Anonymous, we had taken on the USA and UK governments and now we had just bloodied the nose of the largest military alliance in human history.

Several days earlier, on August 11th - The Bay Area Transit or BART took the unprecedented step in the USA of shutting down network cellular and data services normally provided by the repeaters in the stations.

Their motive was not unprecedented however, it was becoming all to mundane for Anonymous. Because BART shutdown the Internet in their jurisdiction to thwart an ongoing police brutality protest taking place in and around the subway stations. Anons were immediately reminded of a slogan Anonymous Egypt had coined as their motto, "If The Government Shuts Down The Internet, Shut Down Your Government". The hashtag #MuBartak began going viral on Twitter. There were DdoS attacks, Defacements, Data Dumps, Doxing - all against BART or its employees and customers. Peter Fein, one of the more infamous founders of the collective called *Telecomix* and I were tasked with managing the IRC and doing media interviews.

The last part would end me up as a guest on DemocracyNow! hosted by the famous Amy Goodman. My fellow guests were none other than Gabriella Coleman, a famous anthropologist who studied hackers and Anonymous, and Peter Fein. And this is how a hacker in Anonymous whose identity is completely unknown makes his first ever television appearance....

Tuesday - August 16, 2011 approx. 3:00 AM ET - "Urban Gorilla Camp" - Mountain View, CA - USA

I was exhausted. I had spent the entire previous day actually marching in what had now become a weekly protest. Every Monday, tens of thousands of people - *many* wearing the now iconic Guy Fawkes Mask (including myself) - would march through the streets of San Francisco disrupting....well, everything. Streets, trains stations, you name it. And the protests were timed to take place during rush hour for maximum disruption. Two local Anons had volunteered to be my transportation and informal body gaurds.

Last night and into the wee hours saw me working feverishly with the technical crew of DemocracyNow!

to stabilize the encrypted tunnel through which I planned to Skype into the show, as well as the software that would encrypt my voice on the fly. It was a delicate house of cards, complicated by the fact that I was working in an outdoor camp using Google's free WiFi. We were quite literally working on it until just before air time. I requested to speak with Amy Goodman off the record in what amounted to a virtual "green room" where guests cooled their heels and awaited being on the air.

Amy Goodman: Hello X, thank you for being on the show today. I know it wasn't easy for you to arrange.

Commander X: No problem, for you I'd do most anything. You are a hero of independent media, especially on the Internet. You innovated most of what we take for granted in Anonymous. I just wanted to tell you, you are my hero.

Amy Goodman: Actually X, you are one of my heroes as well. Thanks again for coming on the air.

I waited in the "green room" for the begining part of the show while Amy interviewed Pete Fein and Biella. Then she began my introduction....

Amy Goodman: This is DemocracyNow! the war and peace report. I'm Amy Goodman. As we talk about what happened at the BART stations in San Francisco and then take this global, we're turning to a closer look at a shadowy hacker activist group known as Anonymous. The group made headlines again this weekend when they hacked into the BART website and leaked the names, phone numbers, and passwords of passengers in retaliation for BART's decision to shut down cell phone service at the four stations last week. Anonymous dubbed the campaign "Op BART".

In recent years online hacktivists who identify with Anonymous have carried out dozens of online Operations. When MasterCard and VISA suspended payment services for WikiLeaks last December hackers with Anonymous took down the websites of both of those credit card giants. Other targets have included Sony, PayPal, Amazon, Bank of America, The Church of Scientology, and the governments of Egypt, Tunisia, and Syria. In recent months law enforcement agencies around the world have begun cracking down on the hackers. In July sixteen suspected members of Anonymous were arrested across the United States. Police in the Netherlands, Britain, Australia, Spain and Turkey have also made arrests over the past year.

We are going to first go to an Anonymous member who joins us now. He is calling himself "X". He was at the BART protest yesterday. He's been up for two days working on the Collective's response to BART's action, shutting down the cell service at four stations. Welcome to DemocracyNow! X. I understand that it's not going to be easy to understand you, because your voice has been encrypted and disguised for security reasons. Tell us what it is that you did in response to BART's actions.

Commander X: Well I think the video you just showed summed it up. We gave them a little taste of their own medicine. We began with a type of campaign we call a "black fax". Then we did an "email bomb", which is basically we took every inbox at the BART organization - several hundred inboxes, and we filled them all with thousands upon thousands of copies of our message of indignation at their actions. And then we took it a step further and we removed the main BART website from the Internet for approximately 6 hours. I'd like to point out that we were cognisant enough to do this on a Sunday when we felt it would be the least inconvenience to the commuter who might need the website for information. So, we did try and think that through.

Finally we went even further, we found a huge security hole in one of their servers. We found them to be terribly insecure actually, and the personal information of over two thousand BART users was just sitting there for the taking. Any twelve year old script kiddie could have gone in and basically grabbed this stuff. So we went ahead and did just that. We took it in order to show the world how you can't even trust your own government to keep this kind of data safe.

Amy Goodman: So in doing this X, you released the personal information on BART riders?

Commander X: Yes, we did.

Amy Goodman: And your thoughts on how it seems like you're going after the individual passengers who might not want that information out there?

Commander X: Well, if we had told them do you think they would have believed us Amy? If we had simply sent them a kind E-Mail message and said 'hi this is Anonymous, we have found all your information unsecure where anybody in the world can take it' do you think they would have believed us? How else do you get the world to respond and secure your information? How else do you get these companies and these governments to keep *your* information safe? I think we got our message across, and I bet you one thing, I bet you they fix that.

Amy Goodman: Let me play a comment on this by the BART spokesman Linton Johnson.

(clip plays)

Amy Goodman: That was BART spokesperson Linton Johnson.

X from the group Anonymous is still on the line with us. X, your response to the BART spokesperson?

Commander X: Yeah well my response is an equal dose of indignation. I would ask BART riders, your listeners, and this BART fellow: *Why* was that information stored on a server with security so lax that it could be taken by any twelve year old script kiddie on the web? It was there for *anybody* to take! At least somebody took it who will use it to send a message to the world that censorship is wrong. And that their information is being held in trust by a government they can *not* trust to keep it safe. They simply don't know what they are doing. I don't know whether BART didn't care to secure that information, or whether they simply don't know *how* to secure that information. But in any case they are a government and they should have known better and they should have done better. If people want somebody to blame, blame the people who they gave that information to in trust and good faith.

We took that information and gave it not only to the world, but we gave it *back* to the people who gave it to BART to let *them* know that they need to fix that. We did that for the *safety* of the passengers. And where's the safety of the passengers when they need help and need to call 911 because they are getting mugged at the dark end of some platform, but they can't because BART has *shut off the cell phone service* over a small protest.

And if this is such a great tactic, why didn't BART use it again? Why didn't they use it against us last night? I was down there, on the platform. We were tweeting, we were surfing. There was no cutting of the cell service. They closed the stations, yes - but how come they didn't cut the cell phone service on us last night? I'll tell you why, because they know they are *wrong*! They know that we got them. And they know if they do it again we will hurt them even worse than we already have.

Amy Goodman: Well let me ask you X: you heard the BART spokesperson say that the FBI is involved right now. Are you concerned about this? There have been a number of arrests of Anonymous members throughout the country in the last month. Are you concerned about this?

Commander X: I am concerned Amy to the extent that I don't want to get caught. And that's why I disguised my voice. I don't want to be hunted. I am literally running from coffee house to coffee house, from city to city, from state to state - to try and avoid this massive multi-million dollar manhunt they have out for Anonymous. And for what? What have we done? We've never harmed a single living being. *Free Topiary!*

While the show had a few more minutes left, I mostly hung out online and listened to Biella talk some more. And then, as if Amy was a prophet - as I closed the laptop and the sun began to rise I looked up and saw a white Crown Victoria with a laptop mounted on the dash board pull away from the street across from my camp.

Monday - September 17, 2011 approx. 12:00 PM ET - Starbucks - Mountain View, CA - USA

Today was the first day of Occupy Wall Street, a protest centered in New York City that in a matter of weeks would include encampments not only in Zuccotti Park, but in over a hundred cities across the USA. And soon Anonymous would be drawn in not only to support Occupy, but OWS and Anonymous would eventually become so intertwined they would be hard to tell apart. The generally accepted history of the Occupy Movement is that on this day an obscure alternative magazine called "Ad Busters" launched OWS, and from there it grew and eventually Anonymous got involved.

I'm going to challenge that established narrative. But before I do, I want to say up front that I am not calling anyone disingenuous. Different perspectives lend themselves to different narratives. But I saw the advent of the Occupy Movement a bit differently than the historic record, and I wanted to share my perspective. In the immediate aftermath of the "Arab Spring", many people in Anonymous discussed how we might transplant this unique phenomenon to the USA.

In a far flung and little known corner of Anonymous there is a group of libertarian "patriot" Anons who among other things ran an Op to try and end the Federal Reserve. I believe in the power of networking so I always made a point to try and connect with these folks when the opportunity presented itself. If you could ignore the more ridiculous tin-foil hat conspiracy theories that abounded within this obscure group within Anonymous, they were actually very friendly and competent hacktivists. Sometime around the first of August in 2011, the general chatter around an "American Fall" to follow the "Arab Spring" began to coalesce into something a bit more refined and serious. The talk centered on trying recreate a "Tahir Style" occupation of the central plaza of Wall Street where the iconic and famous big brass "bull" resides. A test action was planned for one week prior to the formal launch, to gauge what the NYPD reaction might be. And so around September 11, 2011 a small band of proto-occupiers under the name of "Occupy The Bull" spent the day playing around on the bull in the central plaza. Later that night, thirty or so retired to a dark corner of Zuccotti Park and set up camp. The next day they left, and we all retired to IRC to assess how this test protest had gone. I had been drafted to manage the media for the action, and as far as I recall it was then that Ad Busters magazine got involved with promotion of the main action. The name was changed to "Occupy Wall Street", and the rest is public history.

A couple of weeks after the official launch of OWS on Sept. 17th, the main body of Anonymous began to publicly support Occupy Wall Street.

Most were totally unaware that in fact they were supporting something that was essentially a creation of Anonymous. As one of the only media outlets who would give OWS the time of day, Ad Busters appeared to be central to how OWS came into existence. And they were essential in as much as that coverage was needed, especially at the beginning. To be fair, Ad Busters and its readers did physically join the action in NYC and thus from day one had a profound impact on how the Occupy Movement evolved. But in every way that matters, they did not innovate OWS. Rather they joined in, and OWS changed because of their involvement. As far as I could tell from the inside looking out, it was Anonymous that came up with the idea and initial plans that eventually became known to the world as OWS in the USA and the global Occupy Movement.

On this day, as I sat doing media promotion and other tasks for OWS - I already felt like Anonymous was fully a part of what was emerging. And what was emerging was the single greatest challenge in history to oligarchy in the USA. But even I had no idea how this movement would explode across the country in a matter of weeks, creating Occupy encampments in hundreds of cities across the USA. I also had no inkling that day how the Occupy Movement would effect and change Anonymous, or how bound up my own personal fate would become with this "American Fall".

EIGHT

Commander X Captured

"We want to send a message that chaos on the Internet is unacceptable." ~~ Federal Bureau of Investigation

Wednesday - September 21, 2011 approx. 9:00 AM ET - "Urban Gorilla Camp" - Mountain View, CA - USA

My illness had been coming on slowly for weeks. I felt it. I had a vague idea what was wrong with me, but seeking medical attention at this point just wasn't an option. In the past few days, I had declined to the point where I couldn't even walk. I had suffered these collapses in the past. Not often, usually once a year on average. And they were never as severe as this was. My condition is aggravated by stress. And if you've been reading so far the one thing you have to know is stress is what I ate for breakfast. And my health collapse was further exasperated by sleep deprivation and the flu.

The past week the FBI had flooded Mountain View with dozens of agents - I assumed combing the city for me. I had been hiding in a urban gorilla camp along the railroad tracks that ran through the center of town. This afforded me a view of the police station and downtown area while remaining concealed. This morning they literally had me surrounded. I decided not to leave the camp, but in all honesty I'm not certain I actually could have. But I had a little food and water, so I hunkered in to rest and wrap my mind around the fact that I was most certainly about to get arrested by the FBI.

Just after noon I opened up my laptop. First I sent a message to Jay Leiderman telling him to come at once to Mountain View as it was finally time for his debut as the "Lawyer Dude". Then I thought for a long time about what can go wrong with getting arrested by the FBI. I sent an E-mail to the FBI Cyber Crime Division in San Jose with just one short sentence.

"I am not armed. ~~ Commander X"

Then I smoked the last of my weed, and went to sleep.

Thursday - September 22, 2011 approx. 10:30 AM ET - Main Street - Mountain View, CA - USA

As I left the camp, I could see that there were Crown Victoria's fucking everywhere. As I crossed the rail tracks onto Main Street there was an FBI undercover agent clumsily disguised in bermuda shorts and the same cheesey Hawaiian shirts they make them all wear apparently. His gaze never left me as I strolled into town with my day pack slung over one shoulder and my wide brim hat pulled down low. So it was going to be some sort of game. Ok Fibs well fuck you, I can play too.

    I crossed the street and walked boldly into my favorite coffee house and ordered my usual. I took my drink to an upstairs seating area. Thankfully, the entire area was empty. I felt a little relieved and set my stuff down and started slowly walking around the area looking out of the huge old picture windows that over looked the entire central downtown area of Mountain View while I sipped my coffee and thought. There was a way out of this building that they might not be hip to. Next to the bathrooms was an area that looked like a broom closet but was actually a little used stairwell that let out on an alley behind Main Street.

    Just then a young man came up the stairs with a motorcycle helmet in one hand and a coffee in the other. He made a point of sitting a few tables away and facing me. He calmly set down his coffee and helmet, pulled out his smart phone - and snapped my picture bold as can be. Yep okay time to exlore the bathroom and that stairwell. As calmly as I could manage I stood up, grabbed my day pack - and made a point of examining the restroom sign before ducking around the corner. I flew down the stairs without touching a single step. As I exploded into the back ally, a blue Crown Victoria blew by on a side street with a female FBI agent driving. I actually heard her curse as she attempted to slam on the brakes and come back for me.

But she was locked into a morning rush hour traffic pattern, she'd have to double back around - and that could buy me a few precious seconds.

Flat out running was out of the question. In fact, due to my age and health that option has been off the table for a while now. I don't ever run. But I am not above hiding. Furiously I spun around on my heel, scanning for any option. There was a dumpster behind the Mexican restaurant, but the thought of the papers printing pics of my capture with me all covered in food scraps was more than I could bear. I shot between stores back out onto Main Street hoping I could bolt across it into the opposite alley and find better options. As I jogged out onto Main Street, I looked north up Main Street and I saw the now very pissed off female FBI agent in the blue Crown Vic slam her hands on her steering wheel as her partner turned on their flashers and put a blue strobbing bubble light on the roof. The siren went off, and to add to the mayhem, the female agent was laying on the horn and screaming her lungs out. Just then Jay Leiderman drove by me with his mouth hanging open.

The morning traffic was brisk on Main Street and I hesitated bolting through it to get to the other side. That hesitation, as is always the case, is what cost me my freedom - because the female FBI agent had finally had enough and she had simply jumped the sidewalk and was now bearing down on me at speed with pedestrians screaming and leaping out of the way. I spun around on heel again, and saw only an enclosed bus stop that I could duck into. Not much of a hiding place. In a suprisingly calm fashion I stepped into the alcove, set down my day pack and sat down. I calmly lit what I knew would be my last cigarette for at least a few days.

As the blue Crown Vic with "Natasha The Killer Fib" in it screeched to a halt on the sidewalk about twenty-five feet away, a white Crown Vic with two agents pulled up in the street next to the bus stop. And motorcycle guy pulled up behind them. The funniest key-stone cop cluster fuck then began.

"Natasha" leapt from the Crown Vic and was running at me hand on gun before her poor partner could even unbuckle his seat belt. "Commander X, Christopher Doyon! FBI! You are under arrest! FBI!". She had her gun half drawn when a younger FBI agent I recognized as one of the Cyber Crime guys I met briefly in Santa Cruz leapt from the white Crown Vic and ran not into the bus stop where I sat calmly smoking a cigarette and watching. Instead he ran at "Natasha" and practically caught her in his arms. Furiously he whispered at her: "put that thing away, you're scaring the locals" as patrons and barristas alike began to pour out of my favorite coffee house. Most knew me, and were openly asking what I could possibly have done to deserve such attenion from the Federal government. I was sort of starting to wonder this same thing.

Seeing the crowd begin to gather around them, the Cyber Crime agent then touched "Natasha's" jacket and said: "and open your jacket to show your id patch". "Natasha" complied and un-zipped her windbreaker to reveal the iconic yellow letters "FBI" emblazoned across her bullet proof vest. Meanwhile back at my bus stop a whole twenty feet away, Cyber Crime guy's partner had not even bothered to get out of his car, and Motorcycle Dude was leaning against my bus stop. Both were almost laughing. And I just kept smoking my cigarette. I was too sick and tired to find the humor in any of this.

Traffic on Main Street had now come to a complete halt, mostly from rubber-kneckers stopping to gawk at all these FBI agents surrounding this bus stop like Bin Laden himself was inside. Cyber Crime guy calmly strolled into my bus stop and faced me. "You are unarmed" it was more of a statement than a question, Cyber Crime guy had received my communique from yesterday. Good, that would make this measurably easier. I nodded the affirmative to his statement of fact. "Can you tell me your name?" he asked. I looked up at him as I took a slow drag off my cigarette. I calmly exhaled and said: "no offense, but if you don't know who it is you are about to arrest - you are not doing this job right". He chuckled and said: "fair enough, this is your backpack?".

I again nodded the affirmative and he calmly picked it up and handed it to his partner in the white Crown Vic. He stowed it without even checking its contents.

Cyber Crime guy watched me for a few moments as I took several long drags from my disappearing cigarette. As I tossed it into the gutter he stood up straight and said: "are you ready?". Jesus this guy actually sounded sincere too. "Yeah, sure" I said. Gently, almost reverently he took my arm from behind and hand-cuffed me with great care, making certain they were not too tight. Then with just the slightest touch to my arm he led me to get into the back seat of the white Crown Vic. Cyber Crime guy then went around to the other side and got in the back with me as his partner turned off the flashers and eased us out into traffic.

As we began making our way towards San Jose, the FBI agent driving turned on the radio. The agent next to me watched him carefully, and then leaned towards me. "look I know you probably won't talk to us. I get that. I just want to say I'm sorry about this" he said. For the first time today, I was actually suprised by something. Still not entirely convinced this wasn't some bizarre "good cop" routine, I replied a bit testily: "what the fuck do you mean?". "Well, I know you believe in what you do. A lot of people support you. I wish we hadn't had to shut you down" he said with sincerity. Ok so apparently this guy was for real. I softened my tone a few notches and said: "you think you have shut me down? My lawyer is probably like five cars back there behind us. I'll be out in days. All you have done is earn me a six figure book deal". I smiled a kind smile so he would know that while I spoke the harsh truth, it wasn't at his expense. Then he smiled as well and said: "will you say anything nice about me in your book?" he asked. This guy spooked me, he was sympathetic, nice, and he genuinely wanted me to like him - or at least forgive him. I made a point of leaning back looking out the window and seriously considering his request. Then I leaned forward and in a low voice said: "look, you're taking me to lock up. The food isn't fit for dogs.

You buy me lunch, and I'll say *one* nice thing about you personally in my book".

As Jay Leiderman was furiously searching Mountain View for a tailor to sell him a suit fast, I was being booked at the vaunted headquarters of the Federal Bureau of Investigation Cyber Crime Division Headquarters in San Jose, California. They brought me into a room that had a metal folding chair in the middle, a standing work station with two terminals in the corner, and a bare wooden desk and chair in the other corner. Cyber Crime guy took off one hand cuff and attached it to the arm of the chair. Then he and his partner went to the two terminals, which I over-heard them calling "booking" computers. In what has to be one of the funniest things I have ever seen in the not so humerous FBI, these two supposedly highly-trained individuals, essentially the FBI's own hackers - then struggled (unsuccessfully) for the next twenty minutes to boot these machines up. When Cyber Crime guy grumbled about a new secure operating system and reached for a manual under the work station, I coughed and said: "ermmm, if you guys want to uncuff me here, maybe I can give you hand". I was totally joking, and expected a nasty retort. Instead, Cyber Crime guy looked briefly at his partner in a questioning way as if to say "should we?". His partner thought on it for just a moment then violently shook his head no and pulled out that manual himself. And for the first time that day I laughed out loud. Even Cyber Crime guy chuckled at that point.

They asked me if I would submit to questioning. I asked them: "what do you think?". I demanded that I be allowed to call Jay's secretary immediately, I had his card in my pocket - and I desperately needed to let him know which courtroom I would be in later that day. Cyber Crime guy's partner nixed that, it was against protocol. I asked if I could speak to Cyber Crime guy alone. His partner shrugged and went to go get some coffee and hit the head. I turned to Cyber Crime guy as he began to speak and held up my hand. "Let me be crystal clear with you mister.

This has been an interesting game, and I've been super cooperative and I have to admit for a fucking Fib you ain't a half bad human. But if I am not on the phone with Jay's office in exactly five minutes or less, not only will I stop cooperating - I will begin passively resisting. Imagine the fucking headlines tomorrow when the media publishes that Commander X was peacefully taken in Mountain View only to show up in court a few hours later beat to shit. *I WANT MY PHONE CALL NOW!*".

Cyber Crime guy shut up and got out of their fast. Exactly four minutes later I was on the phone to Jay's secretary and gave her the low-down on where to send Jay. Eventually I was transfered to the tender care of the US Marshal's Office at the Federal Court building in San Jose. I was up and down into court at least a couple of times that day as negotiations for my release on bond were painstakingly played out between a still flustered Jay Leiderman (with a new suit at least one size too small) and the cold-blooded fascist of a US Prosecutor. One thing became clear, even the Judge didn't like the smell of my case, and held the Prosecutor's zeal against me with open suspicion. You must bear in mind I was now facing an un-sealed secret Federal indictment that carried penalties of up to 15 years in prison.

Eventually it was worked out that I would have to cool my heals in County lock-up for a week, at which point I was promised another brief hearing and release. As I was sitting in the holding cell alone at the end of a long and exausting day, the door to the cell flew open with a bang, and a huge ass US Marshal hove into view. "I don't know who the fuck you are, but some FBI agent told me to give you this" as he shoved a paper bag through the food slot in the cell bars. The bag contained a foot long roast beef sub, a bag of Dorritos - and a large chocolate milk. The brown paper bag had a smiley face drawn in marker on it.

Ok so....a deal is a deal right? And who knows, maybe Cyber Crime guy will remember and read my book to see if I welched on our "deal".

So here's your one nice thing Cyber Crime guy, for the compassion you showed me that day. You are a good and decent human being, and apparently a man of honor. You seem to care about our world, and have an appreciation for why Anonymous must resist your government. That's your one nice thing. Now, that said - if you read this Cyber Crime guy; the above does *not* relieve you in any way from the moral responsibility of what you and the FBI have done, and what you continue to do - in this relentless and futile war against information activists. In fact, you are even *more* culpable because you *do* know better. So, if you haven't done so already - quit your evil job and do....*anything* else. Because being a decent fellow is simply not enough. There were thousands of very pleasant and gentile Nazis in Germany seventy-five years ago. But they were still fucking fascists, and the so called "good" ones were the *most* guilty.

Saturday - October 1, 2011 approx. 10:30 AM ET - County Court House - Santa Cruz, CA - USA

I had sent out the communique to the media about the Press Conference only two days prior. I simply said that there would be a red "X" in duct tape on the step of the Santa Cruz County Courthouse where I would stand, and the media should set up their equipment accordingly. I told them I would appear between 11:00 AM and Noon, read a brief statement - and then take questions.

    I showed up with a team consisting of Ed Frey local activist and one of my attorneys, radio host Robert Norse, and a local professional videographer who would capture for us my own personal copy of today's proceedings. I was exhausted, I had been giving interviews it seemed non-stop for the few days I had been back at my liberty after finally making bail on the indictment. I had brought copies of the indictment and my arrest warrant for the media.

I had one in my hand as I finished standing around on the top step of the Courthouse prancing around in my pirate hat and crisp new "Free Manning" tee as the media took stock pics of me, and stepped down onto the red "X" where a semi-circle of media had set up in advance as instructed in my communique. Robert Norse held a cell phone in his hand on the other end of which was my none too happy attorney Jay Leiderman, who had done everything he could to talk me out of this stunt. Having failed, he was attending remotely thanks to Robert's assistance.

I took off the pirate hat I was wearing, coughed once to get the journos' attention, and began to speak: "Greetings everyone. I want to thank everyone for coming out to hear what I have to say. I'd like to introduce Ed Frey, an attorney on my legal team. My lead attorney, Jay Leiderman - is joining us from his home in Ventura via cell phone. I would like to state for the public record that this press conference is being held *against* the advice of my legal counsel.

My name is Christopher Doyon. And on last Thursday, September 22nd of this year I was arrested by four or five FBI agents on a street corner in Mountain View, California. I was taken into custody based on this arrest warrant, which was issued because of a previously sealed Grand Jury indictment. Now this Federal indictment alleges certain facts, some which I obviously dispute. And those we'll deal with in court. But I would like to address a couple of facts that I do not dispute.

This document alleges that I am the notorious hacker-activist known to the world as 'Commander X'....

I *am* Commander X.

The indictment further alleges that I am in association with the global internet freedom movement known as 'Anonymous'....

And I say *yes*!

I am immensely proud and humbled to the core to be a part of the idea called *Anonymous*. I say 'proud' because this movement has brought more justice and freedom into this world in the past few years than the United Nations has in *three decades*! And I say 'humbled' because Anonymous is made up of some of the most intelligent and courageous people I have ever known. Many of these wonderful and fiercely dedicated activists are not only fellow freedom fighters, but they are my best friends.

Finally this indictment charges me with certain criminal offenses. in regard to these allegations I can only state at this time that that both my co-defendent Josh Covelli, aka 'Absolem', and myself - are categorically *innocent* of the charges against us and our legal team will provide irrefutable proof of this at our trial.

When we were laying out the plan for today's press conference, one of my friends asked me 'why here?' Why not over at the Federal Courthouse in San Jose?'. I mean that's where it's at, right? And the answer is because this is where it all started. You local journalists know what I'm talking about. *Peace Camp 2010*. For sixty days an intrepid band of homeless people and activists gathered together and occupied this very space. And what was that protest about, Peace Camp 2010? It was about standing up to the rich and powerful few here in Santa Cruz, and to demonstrate a better way of building community.

And it was those powerful few who, fearing the effect that the peaceful protest might have on the coming elections - ordered Peace Camp 2010 to be ended by force, arresting dozens. I myself stand so charged for the physical occupation that took place during Peace Camp 2010. Ed Frey will actually be my lead attorney as I fight those cases. He can also answer all your questions about Peace Camp 2010, which you should be asking a lot more of. Robert Norse is here today. He can speak to his citation for singing a protest song in a legally designated 'Free Speech Zone'.

When justice is denied, and peaceful dissent is forbidden - civil disobedience is the *only logical response*. I may be a street person, but I am *scary smart*. And despite the best efforts of the City, the County - and now the Federal government *I WILL NOT BE SILENCED!* My name is Commander X. And you can damn well expect me."

I took questions for another thirty minutes, and then sat for two additional hours with a local reporter with the Santa Cruz Sentinel newspaper. I finally got some sleep that night, and the next morning found me deep in country at Robert Norse's place. It was beautiful up here in the Santa Cruz mountains. And I found myself at loose ends and not sure what to do next. The FBI had once again stolen *all* of my electronics. To date they now possessed three laptops and four cell phones of mine. Worse yet I was forbidden from possessing any electronics without FBI permission and banned from most social media and chat channels. What the fuck *could* I do even? I started killing some time and watched the movie "Battle In Seattle" a dramatization of the WTO protests in 1999.

And it hit me like a wall. I knew what I would do. I had gained a great deal of notoriety from the arrest, and I was a bit of a folk hero even before the arrest within the Bay Area Occupy Movement. I would travel a circuit of the Bay Area Occupations and just offer to pitch in any way I could, from teaching old-school protest tactics to fund-raising. Even washing dishes or serving food. Fuck the feds, they couldn't stop me from protesting in the streets. And I did end up buying a secret laptop anyway. Fuck you FBI.

NINE

Operation Xport

"The spirit of resistance to government is so valuable on certain occasions, that I wish it to be always kept alive. It will often be exercised when wrong, but better so than not to be exercised at all. I like a little rebellion now and then."
~~ Thomas Jefferson

Wednesday - December 21, 2011 approx. 9:30 PM ET - Starbucks - Santa Cruz, CA - USA

I had received one other message like it. Once, when I was still running from the FBI the last time. I knew they came from a Federal agent, and I strongly suspected now that they were coming from "Cyber Crime" guy. They were always short and terse, and *always* contained some bit of information that was crucial to me. This one was no different. "They are coming for you. You have 24 to 72 hours. You will *not* be released from custody this time". So....damn.

I had since the begining of my run from law enforcment this time around contemplated the possibility that I would be forced to flee the USA. I had dismissed it until now for the simple reason that any such move was a strictly one way trip. The chances that I would ever be able to return home after publicly entering political exile were close to zero. I had determined that I would only consider it as a last resort, if all paths to justice seemed blocked - and the prospect of being shut down and silenced for over a decade in prison seemed imminent.

I had no doubt that the information from my source was accurate. The Feds had had enough, and were coming to shut me down for good. The only real question left was: did I have the courage to follow through on what I knew I needed to do next. Becoming a man without a country is no small matter. I would be hounded and hunted for the rest of my life. And even if I found a country to grant me full and legal political asylum, I would never be able to *leave* that country in my lifetime - except maybe to travel home in a box.

The other question was did I have the physical stamina? The plan we had in place for the Op V Underground Railroad called for the "package" to be slowly transported up the West Coast and be dropped off 30 miles south of the Canadian border where they would hike across an unfenced portion of the international frontier.

Did I have what it took to hike for days through rough mountainous terrain with a seventy-five pound pack on my back? And what about this "Underground Railroad" I had built for Anonymous? Would the individuals I chose play their roles when called upon? Would they risk their own liberty to help preserve another's? For better or worse, I was about to begin learning the answers to my questions. Because my decision was really made the moment I read the dire message from my source. My fate was political exile in Canada....*if* I could get there!

Friday - December 23, 2011 approx. 3:00 AM ET - San Lorenzo River - Santa Cruz, CA - USA

In a hat-tip to the "lulz", I decided to call the attempt to get me out of the USA and into Canada "Anonymous Operation Xport". I had spent a couple of days saying tearful goodbyes to a few local activists I could trust. I remember a particularly difficult conversation with Ed Frey. Ed had put up a sizable chunk of cash towards my bail. When I mentioned this fact he said: "don't let that money get in the way of any decision you have to make, just do what you need to do". Then I sent a pre-arranged coded message to the "operator" of the Anonymous Underground Railroad to let them know they were activated and a "package" was on its way.

The next order of business was to shake the permanent FBI tail I had picked up since my release on bail two months ago. Lately I had been living out of my pack, and when I was at the Occupy Santa Cruz camp I liked to go off to the San Lorenzo river bottom at night to sleep alone. The FBI agent in a white Crown Victoria would park above me on the levyway all night keeping watch over me as I slept. But I laid awake the past few nights and watched carefully, and discovered a chink in this surveillance bubble.

Every morning at approximately 3:00 AM the FBI agent would get out of his car, light a cigarette - and walk away. He usually returned about two hours later.

Tonight, as I lay peeking out of my sleeping bag and watching the ever present white Crown Vic - "FBI Guy" was not cooperating. It was a good half hour past when he usually took his leave. Just when I was ready to give up and catch some sleep, his door opened and he climbed out of his car and stretched. Then as usual, he lit a cigarette and after staring down at me for a few moments - he turned on heel and walked away. I waited patiently for about ten minutes, surreptitiously smoking a cigarette and watching for "FBI Guy" in case he forgot something or otherwise broke his routine and re-appeared. Satisfied, I tore open the sleeping bag and began to move with a purpose. Packing everything up, I slung the pack on my back, grabbed my laptop case - and began working my way east up the San Lorenzo river bottom towards the foothills of the Santa Cruz Mountains. It was tough going. I worked my way over the first ridgeline by Noon, and began my decent towards Route 1 - otherwise known as the Pacific Coast Highway. I arrived at the highway too late in the day to profitably start hitchiking north, so I bedded down at the Wadell Creek rest area.

Saturday - December 24, 2011 approx. 7:00 AM ET - Wadell Creek - Santa Cruz, CA - USA

I had packed up my bedroll, and was staring up the ridge-line at where I knew my old camp was. I briefly considered wasting the time to climb up there one last time. I tried to convince myself maybe there were some useful items there I could grab. The truth was I just wanted to see the place one last time before I left here forever. But I knew there was nothing left of any value up there, and I had already said my good-byes to the place a year ago.

So rather than wasting half a day climbing, I stubbed out my smoke and stuck out my thumb heading north towards San Francisco and the *Anonymous Underground Railroad*. I didn't even realize it was Christmas Eve until I arrived late that afternoon.

My first order of business was to contact my PLF member in the city, Zero. I needed a little money, and a place to rest while I made contact with the first "node" in the Underground Railroad. I knew from our correspondences that he was hanging out at Occupy San Francisco, so I headed down to the encampment. As it turned out, Zero was doing a bit more than hanging out at Occupy San Francisco. He had in fact become nearly indispensable to its day to day operation. Zero was cool like that, and this didn't surprise me. I left messages for him in a bunch of places, then made my way to the edge of the encampment to rest and wait.

Zero finally showed up a few hours later as I was dozing in the late evening sun. He plopped himself down on the grass and exclaimed: "dude what the *fuck* is going on, what's this message I got about an Underground Railroad and you leaving the country?". I spent the next hour smoking some weed and filling him in on the details of the situation. When we finished, he took me to a pizza place he knew of nearby where some of the leaders of Occupy San Francisco liked to hang out in the evening and work on media and stuff. I bought a coffee and some breadsticks with the last of my change as well as Zero's. Then I opened my laptop to make contact with the first "node" of the Underground Railroad.

The first folks in the Underground Railroad in San Francisco was an interesting Anonymous crew called "AnonMedics". They were essentially a street medic bloc with the Anonymous brand. They were very visible at the Bay Area protest scene, with their iconic Anon red cross arm bands and their positively spooky jet black Guy Fawkes Masks. No one knew who these cats were, but everyone knew they were tight as fuck. They also wore matching jet black clothes, and an impeccable black utility belt with various pouches and gear attached.

They had become a fixture at street protests in the Bay Area. Using the pre-arranged protocol I sent a message and then sat back to wait in a secure chat channel. About an hour passed, and someone appeared in the chat.

After what seemed like forever, the person typed to me: "are you the package?". I typed back: "yea, I am". "Where are you?" the AnonMedic asked. I told them the address. "I know the place. Are you alone?" the AnonMedic typed. "No" I replied. "I'm with a member of my crew and some Occupy San Francisco peeps" I typed. There was a long pause. Finally, the AnonMedic typed: "are you ok, do you need anything?". I replied: "I am in decent shape, but I am broke and a bit hungry". There was a much longer pause, well over five minutes passed as I cooled my heels with my eyes glued to the chat tab on my laptop screen. Finally a reply came through. "Go to the counter, tell the wait person you are Brandon Powell. You have a $45.00 tab - buy whatever you want. We'll contact you in two hours" and with that the AnonMedic left the chat channel. Damn, these guys were good!

I did as instructed, and then since I could see no reason not too - I used the balance of my "tab" to feed the entire Occupy San Francisco crew, Zero included. I even had enough for a couple of pitchers of beer. Still tired from my travels that day, but feeling much better - I sipped my beer and prayed that my AnonMedic angel kept their word and returned. I was not disappointed. "Look across the street, do you see the grey mailbox on the sidewalk" the AnonMedic typed upon returning to the chat channel. I looked up and through the front window of the pizza place and sure enough, there under a street light was a grey mailbox. "Yes, I see it" I typed back. "In 45 minutes go out there and stand next to it. Put your pack on the ground at your feet. Do you have a Guy Fawkes Mask with you?" the AnonMedic asked. As it turns out I did and I said so. "Good, put the Mask on top of your backpack and wait. Say nothing to anyone."

A car will come by, if you see a Mask in the back seat - get in" and with that the AnonMedic was gone from the chat channel.

Forty-five minutes later saw me standing there under the street light next to a mailbox on a San Francisco street with my pack at my feet and my Mask showing through the open top. I felt slightly ridiculous, but also I felt a bit like I was in an old spy novel. I'll admit to being a bit scared. A car drove by slow, the passenger obviously checking me out. I tried not to look at them, and kept my hat pulled low over my face as I chain smoked. The car never slowed, and turned down a side street without pausing. I sighed and lit a smoke. Maybe it was them, and they didn't like what they saw. Maybe it was the fibs. Who the fuck knows, and I was scared. This shit was way too "spy thriller" type action for my tatses. I am more of a "hack the world from a dark corner of a coffee house" type of revolutionary.

Minutes rolled by, and I was feeling a bit foolish, not to mention exposed. Just as I flicked a butt into the gutter, I felt more than heard a presence behind me. I turned slowly, and what I saw caught me by surprise. She was tall, slim. Dressed in that iconic and impeccable black body suit, but sans the utility belt - and of course she wasn't wearing a Mask on a city street. She said nothing, just made a point of noticing the Mask peeking out of my backpack, and then she turned slowly and calmly walked around the corner. I zipped up my pack, threw it over one shoulder - and heart pounding I tried to follow her with as much dignity as I could muster.

As I rounded the corner, a non-descript older model four door sedan, it might have been an old Impala - was quietly idling. The young lady who had approached me was already sitting in the passenger seat quietly conferring with the driver. The back door on the sidewalk was wide open. I approached somewhat cautiously, and sitting on the seat was one of the AnonMedic's iconic jet-black Guy Fawkes Masks. I gently and reverently moved it aside, tossed in my pack first - then quickly slid in and closed the big old door with as much grace as I could muster.

I was literally out of breath, more from the adrenaline than from the exertion. The driver turned from talking to the girl, and put the car into gear and smoothly pulled away. That's when I noticed in the rearview that the driver was a girl too! So....were *all* the now famous and extremely mysterious AnonMedics women? All males suffer from residual mysogyny, if they are honest. And I cop to the fact that this possibility never dawned on me. I was pleasantly amazed, and willing to swallow the shame of my surprise to enjoy the wonder of what was happening to me.

Because the moment I climbed into that car, I was in the *Anonymous Underground Railroad* that I myself had created. There were strict rules and protocols. I had worked hard at this and recruited in person and online the finest individual activists I could find. They had been drilled relentlssly in the protocol so they could memorize it and leave no electronic foot-print. And the "package" had rules too. I had to be ego free, no pulling rank because of who I was or thought I was. I was to trust the activists in whose care I was with absolute and instant obedience. They in turn would use every resource at their disposal to do two things. Keep me safe, and get me to the next "node" on the Underground Railroad. Only the "Operator" of the Underground Railroad was supposed to know all the nodes, and would direct the "package". However I did have one slight advantage there, I built the thing - so I had a pretty good idea which "nodes" my "Operator" would activate.

My "Operator" was a fine if eccentric Anon from eastern Canada who went by "OpNoPro". And my destination ultimately was an area approximately thirty miles south of the Canadian border, where I would then be on my own to hike for days through the wilderness and across an unfenced portion of the international boundry. However, it was winter. So OpNoPro had instructions to get me there slowly, with long stops along the way. That way I would at least arrive at the border in early Spring of '12.

It would still be cold as shit and rough going, but I was born and raised in the back-woods of Maine so I knew with the right gear it was do-able.

The driver looked up at me in the rear view mirror apprisingly, as her partner turned to me in the passenger seat and said: "you seem a bit scared, you ok?". I laughed. It was completely inappropriate and unprofessional, but I laughed and laughed until I was choking. By the time I was done both girls were trying not to giggle also, and failing. Finally I choked out: "are you all girls? All the AnonMedics?". The Anon in the passenger seat said: "that's not appropriate to ask. But at least two of us are!" and she smiled so I knew the rebuke was a gentle one. "You ok to be briefed?" the driver asked me. I nodded, and took a deep breath to compose myself.

"We can't take you to either our personal space, or our local AnonMedic space. For the next couple of days while we work out some details you'll be staying at a safe-house we have arranged for you in Oakland. We're driving there now. The house is being used by a lot of people and it will be crowded, but you'll be safe and secure there. Just don't talk to anyone there about Anonymous. Those there who need to know will, no one else should. You understand?" the driver looked up at me in her rear-view as she finished. I nodded, too impressed to even speak. Holy shit these people were tighter activists than I will ever be, was all I could think.

The neighborhood we had entered in Oakland was fairly well heeled. The car stopped in front of what appeared to be a gated mansion, old - but not disheveled at all. It seemed to have been sub-divided into at least three units, apartments. It was at least a hundred years old and in that sort of unique Bay Area Victorian style you see a lot in San Francisco especially. Then the car simply drove away. I knew better at least than to inquire if my companion had some other way home. I zipped my lip, and we approached the wrought-iron gate. From the shadows emerged a *huge* young black man wearing full camo fatigues, a bandana, and carrying a baseball bat.

This cat was clearly not happy to see us, and expressed this viscerally by growling through the bars: "get. the. fuck. lost.". Yeah ok I heard him, I say we go right? No way. My companion was not a *small* woman by any measure, and obviously had the heart of a warrior. She smiled and leaned her shoulder towards the bars. Slowly she reached up to a square of black velcro on her upper left arm, and ripped it open. Underneath was the iconic full color logo of the AnonMedics. Jesus fucking christ, there was just no end to how tight these people had their shit together. Fuck me....

Instantly the demeanor of the man at the gate changed. He went from being a growling street thug with a bat to being almost soldier like towards my companion. And to be clear, my girl out ranked this dude by a bit. He said: "they told us you were coming. This the 'package'?" he pointed at me. "Yes." my companion replied. He turned to me as he let us both through the gate and re-attached a large chain and lock to it: "they would like to talk to you upstairs". My companion intervened: "he's exausted and hungry. He's not a performing circus bear." she said with a scowl. "Hey look I feel you, but as I heard it this ain't a request. Boss wants to meet the famous hacker dude he's putting up." the gate-keeper replied as he started leading us up a flight of stairs. My companion went to dig in her heels and I stayed her. "Look it's cool, I can sing for my dinner if I have to. Let's just go get it over with" I said gently.

We were led into a top floor unit. As we entered the room there were three other men and one woman already there. To be clear, myself and my companion were the only white people in the room. All the others had various pieces of camo clothing on, and utility belts hung heavy with mysterious pouches and tools. There were no weapons present other than baseball bats and knives. No firearms. The air hung heavy with a thick cloud of marijuana smoke. The room had a table with four chairs and various stuffed furniture around the walls. Everyone leaned forward to get a close look at the "package".

A man who was clearly the "Boss" our gate-keeper had spoke of slowly rose to his feet and came up to face me.

He stared me hard in the eyes for what seemed an eternity. He said not one word. Then he turned around, grabbed an open beer from the table and slowly sat back down. He coughed, drank some beer - and said: "Anonymous and the AnonMedics have been our best and most important allies. They have never asked anything in return for the help they give us. This...."package", is under my roof and under my protection. Are we clear?" he turned and slowly took in the faces of his companions, including our gate-keeper. As one they nodded and grunted their assent, and then as if the show was over they just went about what ever they were doing before we arrived.

Our gate-keeper then led us back down the stairs to the bottom floor unit. He came in and looked around the large living room type area. It was packed with activists camping out, and for the first time since I had arrived at this "safe-house" I saw other white people. And I could tell right away they were from Occupy Oakland. Things were beginning to make a little sense, but I still had some questions that I needed answers to. Our gate-keeper went to a particularly comfy looking corner area of the large room where three Occupy Oakland folks had laid out bedrolls, busted open backpacks - and made them selves at home. "Pack all this shit up and get out, you have five minutes." he growled at them. They didn't hesitate a moment to comply and within minutes I had been installed in this area. It afforded me some measure of privacy, and I was relieved to finally drop my pack and laptop case.

Our gate-keeper turned to me and said: "can you really hack shit?" he asked. As I shook his hand I said: "yeah, at least the feds think so anyway". He laughed, and slapped me on the shoulder. "Boss says you're the real deal that's good enough for me. But that's some off the hook shit, that hacking stuff". He turned to my companion and asked: "you need anything else?". I intervened: "actually yeah, I need to talk to my friend. In private." I said.

Our gate-keeper shrugged and pointed to a back door: "the back yard, that's about the only place in the house not crawling with Occupiers".

Without hesitating I took the lead and strode through the door as I shook out a much needed cigarette. My companion followed me behind an old utility shed, where a couple of old buckets made convenient seats. "Sit" I said, "let's have a chat". She seemed like she wanted to leave, but reluctantly she sat. "Do you know who I am?" I asked her. She hesitated, then answered: "yes, you are Commander X. We're not supposed to know or care who the "package" is, but when our node was activated we suspected it might be you". I nodded and said: "what's going on here, what is this place?" I asked. "The package is supposed to be given only that information which is...." I held up my hand to stay her. "Don't quote the protocols to me, because I have a revelation for you. *I wrote the protocols*. I created this entire network. I just never dreamed I would be the first one to use it. As for need to know...." I paused and looked around me and waved my hand "....I think I need to know".

My AnonMedic sighed, then went on to explain that this house was a foreclosed property that had been seized in protest by a local Black Militant group in tangent with Occupy Oakland. The seizing of empty buildings was a tactic that I had actually helped introduce to the Occupy Movement in Santa Cruz, when myself and a small group of local Anarchists seized an empty Wells Fargo Bank building. It was a fairly provocative tactic that really pissed off the authorities. The tactic had instantly swept the Occupy camps across the nation. And DHS never forgot exactly which Anarchist had a part in starting it all. In fact it may have been DHS that yanked the FBI's chain to have me brought back in. "And you think *this* is a good safe house for me?" I asked her. She bristled slightly at that, and replied: "we're doing the best we can. There was not a lot of time to prepare. But yes, this place may seem weird but you are totally safe here. Once the big guy here gives his word, these people would kill and die to protect you".

I wasn't at all certain I was ready to have people doing either of those things on my behalf, but I let it slide. "Ok, I trust you" I said as I stubbed out my smoke. My companion gave me a bag of food from her small black backpack, and pushed forty dollars into my hand. "Just lay low here, stay out of people's way. We'll be back for you in a few days. We'll have something more comfortable, and permanent then." and then she left. I actually never saw any of the AnonMedics again. They activated the next "node" in the Underground Railroad and handed me off. But I will never, ever forget these people. They were so brilliant and so *scary* organized. With Anons like these in the world, the bad guys should be very afraid indeed!

Monday - December 26, 2011 approx. 9:00 PM ET - Oscar Grant Plaza "Occupy Oakland" Camp - Oakland, CA - USA

When the instruction/order to move to my next "node" came, it was with little warning. I was told that my presence was no longer desired, and that I should make my own way to the Occupy Oakland main encampment in Oscar Grant Plaza and wait there for someone to come for me. I was given a recognition code word, which I was told was also the name of the individual in charge of my next "node". Then I was shown out the door and the gate was locked behind me. When I asked for directions, my old buddy the "gate-keeper" simply pointed up the street and said: "it's that way".

It was *not* a short walk, especially through a hot downtown Oakland with seventy-five pounds on my back and a laptop case in my hand. But I got there, a little after noon. As Occupy encampments go, I had visited quite a few - and Occupy Oakland in Oscar Grant Plaza was second only to OWS in Zuccotti Park itself. It was a vast camp, with hundreds of tents and other temporary structures.

It had an amazingly complex and efficient infrastructure including a full kitchen that fed non-stop almost 24/7, an information booth and library, a day care center for the children living in the camp, a clinic with a full corp of trained street medics, including you guessed it - a contingent of AnonMedics. The encampment hummed with activity at all hours day and night as activists used it as a base of operations from which to plan and execute actions all over the city of Oakland under the Occupy banner.

Occupy Oakland was also the most diverse of all the Occupy camps, in that it had so many different transgressive groups working side by side with little to no friction and a high level of cooperation. Black urban militants worked side by side with mostly white Black Bloc Anarchists. Hippies built structures with homeless veterans. Yuppies pissed off at the economic or environmental injustices paid no mind to the needle exchange that was set up at one end of the camp. Occupy Oakland was living proof a community could be chaotic, anarchic - and yet still be peaceful and thrive.

Prior to my arrest by the FBI in Mountain View, I had spent a great deal of time at Occupy Oakland, and I was well known and liked in the camp. On the night the Oakland Police shot a young three-tour-of-duty Iraq veteran protester named Scott Olsen, I was standing on one side of the street from him in Mask and pirate hat streaming, and award winning CNN journalist Amber Lyon was standing opposite me. I will never forget the moment it happened. The police line was advancing, and they had fired numerous vollies of....*everything* at the protesters. Myself and Amber had taken opposite sidewalks in an attempt to stay out of the line of fire and keep covering the confrontation.

Scott Olsen broke away from the retreating protesters. He had a bandana pulled up over his mouth, not so much to hide his face as to try and breath with all the CS gas in the air. He slowly approached the police line with his hands in the air. He pulled open his camo jacket to show he had no weapon and continued to slowly walk towards the line.

It was one of those moments at protests where you know something iconic, something historic even - is about to happen. But it will almost assuredly come at the expense of this young man whoever he was.

As he stopped walking approximately fifty feet from the police line I saw that he was also wearing a Veterans For Peace shirt. He knew, and I knew - that the cops could see it. That and his camo clothing and his incredibly courageous stance said it all. This was a veteran who had seen combat in one of the most violent war theatres in human history, he was not going to be afraid of police while peacefully standing in the streets of his own city.

There was a moment....I don't know if it was just me or if others felt it. Everything seemed to go into slow motion. I saw Amber Lyon struggling to bring her camera up as she realized what was about to happen as well. The protesters who had retreated about a hundred feet down the street even seemed to go quiet and expectant. I remember thinking just before it happened, *no* - surely not. Surely *not* in the USA. And then with blinding speed the world cracked audibly and it happened. One of the cops in the line growled like a wild beast and stepped forward with a *huge* fifty milimeter military grade grenade launcher and fired what we would later figure out was a bean bag round at point blank range straight into Scott Olsen's face and dropped him unconscious like a sack of rocks in the street with blood gushing from his forehead. He was immediately carried from the field by a cordon of street medics, with a gaping hole in his forehead.

It was one of the most iconic moments in the history of the Occupy Movement. For those who were actually there, the hatred of the government seared into our souls from that moment will fuel our resistance to this system for the rest of our lives. That was the moment I lost all faith in reform within the USA and realized it really was a rogue regime that needed to be removed from power. The next day, the famous film maker Brian Knappenberger would finally catch up with me to film me for my part in what would eventually become the iconic full length motion picture documentary *We Are Legion*.

I was filmed as four helicopters hovered over head and about five thousand people held a General Assembly and decided to shut down *all* the West Coast shipping ports for a day in honor of Scott Olson, who was in critical condition and a coma but expected to survive. A protest that did happen and cost the USA economy over a billion dollars. As much of the history of the Occupy Movement is bound up in Occupy Oakland as it is in OWS in Zuccotti, maybe more.

    I found a grassy spot in the shade near enough to the Information Booth that I could keep an eye on what amounted to the "main street" of this little village called Occupy Oakland. Afternoon slipped into night as I lounged around on the grass, napped, smoked cigarettes - and waited patiently. So far the only thing that had changed was the volunteer in the info booth. A white hippy girl had left and was replaced by a dour looking young black man who seemed to stare at me more than he should. Whatever, this was like my second home in the Occupy Movement so I was okay with being noticed by a few. As it grew solidly dark and I was just starting to wonder if I should just roll out for the night, a group of young Anarchists appeared in the central area. They were obviously a group of friends, and they chatted, played hackey sack, smoked weed - and totally paid no mind to me at all.

    As I put out my last smoke, and thought about dropping my stuff at the Info Booth and going to buy more, one of the young people seemingly just gathered there socializing broke away from the group and approached me. He offered me a whole pack of smokes, and asked me if I'd like to go grab a beer. He didn't use the code word, so I said I had to decline as I was waiting on some friends. He thought about that for a moment and then replied: "well, a lot of people go to this bar you know. It's just around the corner and quite popular. I have a *theory* you might meet your friends there". And with that he turned on heel, waved good bye to his friends - and started walking across Oscar Grant Plaza.

As I scrambled to follow him, I noticed the dour young black man who had been manning the Info Booth motion another person to take his place and he fell in behind me as I followed *Theory*.

We walked only about a block through downtown Oakland in total silence. Theory entered the bar and went straight to a set of stairs in the back. Using a key he took from his pocket, he unlocked a black door that led into an upstairs seating area that over-looked the main floor through a glass window. There were only a few tables up here, and none were occupied. Within moments a waiter appeared. Theory quickly ordered some hot food and a pitcher of beer and the waiter left without a second glance. He turned to me and smiled: "so, the infamous Commander X is the *package*. I should have known!". He proceeded to give me a bear hug. As he released me I set down my stuff and looked around, especially out the picture window that let out on the main floor of the establishment.

"Not to worry" Theory said. "It's one way glass. This room is normally rented out to private groups, but the bar owner supports Occupy Oakland and lends it to us for meetings. We won't be disturbed, you're safe here. Have a seat let's get you fed" he said as the food and beer arrived. As we sat I caught Theory's eye and glanced at our black brother who was very enthusiastically attacking the food and beer. "X, allow me to introduce Jimmy. He's a solid part of Occupy Oakland. He's also a part of our little Underground Railroad. We're setting you up with a more long-term solution for a safe-house, but we need you to lay low in Oscar Grant Plaza for a few days while we organize it. Jimmy and his crew are going to keep you safe and look out for you" he said and turned to Jimmy. Jimmy wiped his mouth, nodded at me - and said: "homeboy needs to lose that beard and ponytail. Everyone in Occupy Oakland knows this cat" and he went back to enjoying what was obviously some rare hot restaurant food for this seasoned Occupy warrior.

"We have that covered X, let's start with this" Theory opened up a day pack and took out a pair of electric clippers.

He reached under the table and plugged them in, then he got up and retrieved a small waste-paper basket from the corner of the room and came over and set it between my feet. "Make yourself look different" he said with a smile. I looked around. I was in a private room in a public bar in downtown Oakland and about to sheer myself like a sheep. The strangeness was palpable at this point. Theory got the feeling too, and smiled at me as he grabbed some of the food and beer for himself.

    The beard came off easy enough. The ponytail was another matter, I had to settle for hacking about a foot of it off with my hunting knife. "Not to worry X, we have more goodies for you" as he pulled out a dull brown used hoodie and tossed it across the table at me. Classic hacker fashion. I pulled it on. Theory smiled and handed me a pair of new sunglasses. I laughed as I completed my disguise by sliding them on. I turned to Jimmy my new body gaurd and stuck out my tongue. "Yeah, that will do. Just don't be giving any speeches or causing a fuss like you usually do here" and he actually smiled at me. Jimmy and I would get along, and I was so scared at this point speeches were the last thing on my mind. Theory gave me a fist full of cash, maybe fifty bucks - and then led me and Jimmy back to the Occupy Oakland camp.

Saturday - December 31, 2011 approx. 9:30 PM ET - Oscar Grant Plaza "Occupy Oakland" Camp - Oakland, CA - USA

Theory had blown through the camp earlier in the day to let me know that they would be moving me that night to a new safe-house. The only other detail he left me with is it was not in Oakland, but outside of the city somewhere - and that we would be driven there by the leader of the next "node" in the Underground Railroad. As the time for the pick-up approached, some sort of confrontation between Occupy Oaklanders and the police developed.

Theory arrived with folks in tow just as the cops started popping off the tear gas and flash-bang grenades. Chaos rained down around us with people running in every direction and screaming as a full on assault on Occupy Oakland unfolded. The three of us ran, with me and Theory following the new guy he brought with him. I had no idea where we were going, but I had no problem keeping up as we dodged down an alley to try and avoid another phalanx of riot cops coming through the downtown area heading towards Oscar Grant Plaza.

Finally we came out on a street that seemed to be away from the fray, although we could still hear the street battle un-folding in the distance. "Just another day at Occupy Oakland" Theory said with a laugh as we leaned up against a parked car gasping and heaving. The new guy we followed, who I assumed was my new contact - smiled and said: "yeah well this is my car, I say we get the hell out of here fast". Neither Theory nor I needed to be told twice and we jumped in. As we sped away I took one last look out the back window and realized a feeling I would be having a lot of in the future, namely the sense that I was never going to see this city that I loved so much ever again. This really was a one way trip, and it was sinking in. I would always be saying good bye to people and places, because I could never go home.

We drove on the freeway, north east out of Oakland and into Richmond. On the ride, the new guy Peter briefed me on the new safe-house. Peter was part of a militant splinter group of Occupy Oakland. What he and his team did was some of the most interesting and innovative work I had encountered so far in the Occupy Movement. Peter and his team first went out at night and scouted foreclosed residential properties in the Richmond area. When they found one suitable to their needs, they then gathered volunteers to occupy the property. They could be homeless folks, protesters, even curious college students. The volunteers would then be trained in how to legally occupy the residence.

The lights, water and gas would be turned on - and the residents would be responsible for paying those bills. The bills were important, because legally that meant the occupants could not be forcibly removed until after an expensive and time-consuming eviction process in civil court has played out. Of course this strategy had only a modest level of success, as the Richmond Police would not hesitate to raid one of these "political squats" and evict everyone with force. Peter and his team had set up over a dozen of these guerrilla occupations, and went out two nights a week to either scout or set up more.

The particular one of these houses I was being taken to was their flagship and base of their seditious operations. The entire neighborhood loved the squatters, I was told - and regularly covered for them if the cops came sniffing about. They had an organic garden, brewed their own beer, and even had a chicken that laid a few eggs. I had brought along a portable cellular WiFi modem, and offered to fire it up and provide Internet for the house while I was there. I was informed that to make things more comfortable, the other reseidents of the squat had been informed of who I was and why I would be staying there. They were a solid, tight, and loyal crew I was reassured - so no worries.

    The house was very nice, and in an upscale neighborhood in Richmond. The neighbor lady next door looked up from her gardening and gave Peter a warm smile and a wave of a gloved hand as he pulled up into the driveway. "See, I told you - all the neighbors know what we are about and they love us!" Peter exclaimed as he got out of the car. He led me inside, introduced me to the other residents who were home at the time, and then showed me my room in the house. "We thought you might like a little privacy" he said with a smile. Everything in the house works, including the shower. But no hot water yet, we're working on that. I'll leave you to settle in and rest. I'll knock in a few hours with some dinner". And with that he and Theory went off to confer on other important Occupy business.

As I set up my laptop, a chicken walked in and jumped up on the desk and began carefully examining my computer.

Friday - January 13, 2012 approx. 8:30 PM ET - "Safehouse" - Richmond, CA - USA

It had been a long day. Since arriving I had slowly turned my "room" in the safe-house into an Anonymous Command Center, with multiple computer workstations, maps of the world and the Bay Area on the walls, and tons of memes and Anonymous iconography as well. I was using it myself to continue my work in various Anonymous Ops, and also using it as a base for local Anons to meet, plan, and execute online Operations in support of Occupy Oakland. Or sometimes, just make up and print a flyer. But the space was set up, and it was appreciated and well utilized. At the moment my focus was on supporting the massive protests in Nigeria dubbed "Occupy Nigeria" with an Anonymous Operation I had launched called appropriately "Op Nigeria".

I had received an interesting encrypted message that day from a hacker I knew in one of the Anonymous related crews. Apparently word of my run towards the border was begining to leak online. There were vague rumors. He wanted me to know, and offered me a gift if I ever needed it. Seems his crew was able to break into the NCIC computer system and delete BOLO's and arrest warrants. But, I was warned - it was only good for a few hours at best. I filed it away for future reference, as I certainly could envision many scenarios where I might just need such a "magic trick".

Tonight pretty much all of Anonymous had gathered online in Twitter and IRC to watch and comment on a much anticipated CNN Special called "Inside Anonymous" produced by award winning investigative journalist Amber Lyon. The channels all got real quiet as the episode began.

This was Anonymous, and they were braced to not only hate it - but to troll its poor producer Ms. Lyon into oblivion in the process. But it wasn't to be. The piece was brilliant, inciteful and dramatic. Amber Lyon had won the day, and the hearts of Anonymous - in less than forty-five minutes. To my mind the most brilliant line was when Amber was describing the connection between Anonymous, Guy Fawkes - and the infamous *Gunpowder Plot*. "Instead of gunpowder, Anonymous uses their key boards to effect social change" Amber said in a voice-over. Brilliant stuff, I was so impressed that I did something I have never done before. I reached out to a journalist unilaterally.

Tapping on her Twitter handle I discovered to my suprise that Ms. Lyon was already following me. That made things easier, as I could simply DM her - which I did: "Amazing piece on us, great job. You won the hearts and minds of Anonymous tonight. Let me know if you want to *really* go inside Anonymous." I sent. I got a reply back in seconds, apparently Amber was online and monitoring the reaction to her piece airing in real-time. "Thank you so much! Deal, where and when?" she replied. I sent her a link to an IRC server where we were running #OpIran and #OpNigeria. I walked her through securing her namespace and obtaining a Vhost to hide her location data. Then I proceeded to have one of the more interesting conversations I have ever had with a journalist. I began by explaining some of the players in the #OpIran channel we had based out of for our convo.

Commander X: Arash is an Iranian ex-pat. TarenCapel is a PLF Commander and part of Anonymous UK. The three of us started Operation Iran in Feb. of 2011. I think...or March, something like that. If you need exact dates of stuff, I will need time to look it up in our archives. Which are vast and not well organized.

Amber Lyon: Thanks again for all the help. Is this where you spend most of your time during the day?

Commander X: Welcome to IranServ, we don't do Lulz here we wreck dictators. I have about a half dozen or more communications channels I monitor, and I am online and in about two dozen channels on all three secure Anonymous IRC servers. TarenCapel has been informed of your presence on this Server, and he will watch out for you. Ask him if you need anything. I have verified your identity, so you are good to go.

Amber Lyon: So when can I come visit you and do a profile on your life, the PLF, and future Anonymous Ops?

Commander X: Lulz. You're bold aren't you.

Amber Lyon: I think you have a fascinating story that I would like to tell if you give me the permission to do so. You can set the terms.

Commander X: Brave as well.

Amber Lyon: Its become so difficult to do our jobs as of late. It drives me crazy!

Commander X: Yes I am very angry at the moment.

Amber Lyon: So am I.

CommanderX: I hate it when people kill people for no reason, and especially when I am working with them. I tend to take such things quite personally. What is it with you, that I feel this need to unburden myself so. You are a strange one, TarenCapel is right you need watching!

Amber Lyon: What do you mean I need watching? Confused.

Commander X: So am I. I do not usually get so...chatty, with reporters. Never mind, anyway....

Amber Lyon: That's ok...it's my midwestern upbringing. People often feel comfortable talking with me because I am real with them.

Commander X: TarenCapel thinks you are dangerously cute and nice, the persians mistrust the media because they have been very unkind to the cause of Iranian Freedom. But no worries TC likes you, he is...it's his job to be suspicious of everything.

Amber Lyon: I'll take it as a compliment that he likes me.

Commander X: You must understand how afraid we all are, all of Anonymous and the whole underground.

Amber Lyon: What are you most afraid of?

Commander X: They are hunting us like dogs on three continents. Pain. I can't stand pain. I want to die clean, no prison or pain. I fear pain the most, prison the second most. Death the least of all. In fact death I would welcome if it would save others from it.

Amber Lyon: Who are you willing to die for? Why are you willing to die for people you don't know? Why do you care so much for them?

Commander X: The innocent, the oppressed and disenfranchised - the voiceless masses of beautiful humanity. Any of them, all of them - to save them from the butchers I would easily die a thousand deaths. Because they are beautiful. They are humans, we are humans - because their pain and suffering is my own.

If I must weep for them then god damn it I will also fight for them as well. And die if it is necessary. Though lets be clear, I hope it will not be. 10,000 children a day die of starvation while less than 1% have control over 40% of the wealth of the world. Strip out the numbers and the spin of that statement, whats left? A mother with a dead baby in her arms. And some rich fuck with ten hookers and a thousand dollar a plate meal. I am going to fix that fucking shit, the hard way. We will take the fat fuck, lock him up and take his wealth and feed the fucking children.

Amber Lyon: You have an incredible sense of empathy. Not many people can feel a stranger's pain .... truly feel it.

Commander X: I feel more than pain. I feel an unquenchable rage. And that is always dangerous but it is made more so Ms. Amber by the fact that I am an extremely powerful individual. And I know it.

Amber Lyon: Do you think the U.S. gov fears your power?

Commander X: Thats an interesting question. Overall I think they are coming to a begrudging respect.

Amber Lyon: Seems like you have allies in all corners as of late, people sick of helplessly watching as others get ruined by corporate and government corruption. Have they ever come close to finding you?

Commander X: They *caught* me Amber.

Amber Lyon: I know, but recently.

Commander X: Twice this time around. Since I escaped their little bubble and bolted. They have no idea where I am now.

Amber Lyon: Have any other Anons escaped to Canada?

Commander X: I can't discuss that.

Amber Lyon: Ok. understood.

Commander X: I am prepared to consider allowing you access to me, as you have requested. I may even be prepared to allow you to record as I move from safe-house to safe-house, and perhaps even allow you to record my exit from the USA. Which will be fairly dramatic. However the conditions are not mine to make or set.

Amber Lyon: I want to come with you. I know it sounds crazy. But I would like to be there.

Commander X: You frighten me. I consulted those in whom I have entrusted my life and liberty. This is their decision not mine because it is they who have risked everything to keep me safe. We have a model for this, we granted CBS similar access. Amber, you must come alone. You would need to basically place yourself in Anonymous and my hands. But it can all be arranged.

Amber Lyon: Ok. Understood. I've noticed you are a superhero to them.

Commander X: There will be things that we will ask you to do, things that can help us acertain if you are being followed.

They will be normal things not weird, but you must follow instructions exactly. Any deviation and they WILL call it off and move me.

Amber Lyon: Ok, will do. I'd also like to know if I am being followed.

Commander X: Level with me why do you want to do this so much?

Amber Lyon: Because this, all of it...it's an amazing story that should be told.

Our conversation actually went on for two more hours and ranged over topics as disparate as the situation in Bahrain to what I do for fun (not much). When it was finally over in the wee hours of the morning I was not only physically exausted but emotionally drained as well.

Wednesday - January 25, 2012 approx. 4:30 PM ET - "Safehouse" - Richmond, CA - USA

The day began normal enough. The safehouse quietly buzzed with its daily routine while I worked through my various daily tasks within Anonymous. There were two other residents with me, both college students. When disaster struck, as usual it was with no warning....and it was wearing a Richmond Police uniform. I got up from my computer to stretch and as I did I pulled back the make-shift curtain on the window in my room to let in a little more light. As I did that, I saw for just a flash in the alley below - a Richmond Police officer. He was skulking around on the side of the building, and he had his gun drawn. He didn't see me as I gently let the curtain fall back into place.

I didn't hesitate, but moved with a purpose. Within less than a minute I had sent a coded message via a friend to the hacker who a month before had claimed he could work magic with the NCIC system. "Tell him now, please" was all I sent. He'd know what I meant. Then I shut down the computers in the room and began a careful examination for any way out of this room, or a place to hide. That's when I heard a crash in the living room, something like breaking china. I carefully nudged my door open and looked out.

There was one of the residents, a female college student. There was a broken plate of food on the floor at her feet and she appeared to be fixated on the picture window in the living room, which I could not see from this angle. Without breaking her gaze, she quietly and calmly said: "I have a gun pointed at me". Suddenly the cop who was on the front porch and pointing a gun at this poor young lady began to shout: "open the front door! Open the fucking front door or we'll break it down! Do it now!" he practically screamed. He sounded insane, to be honest. "What should I do?" the girl asked, again without breaking her gaze on the officer holding her at gun-point through the picture window. "Keep your hands in plain sight, and slowly go open the door" I replied.

As the bolt lock clicked, the door slammed in and the cop came storming in with his gun inches from the young ladies face. "Get on the ground! Lay down on the fucking ground! Do it now!" he screamed with spit flying from his lips. With my hands at my side, I calmly stepped into the room and said: "put that fucking gun away. You know god damn well these kids are protesters and not armed. Put that fucking thing away" I said with a touch of anger. He swung around and pointed the gun at my head: "jesus christ how many people are here? Get on the fucking ground *now*!" he shouted at me. "Or what, dude? Are you going to fucking shoot a bunch of unarmed people in their own home?" I shouted back. All at once two other officers swarmed in and we were both thrown to the floor, handcuffed, and led out into the front yard and then lined up face to the garage door. They had already found the other kid, hiding behind the chicken coup in the backyard.

They searched us, and found no ID on any of us. Just when I was starting to think I might wiggle out of this, one cop came out of the house with a day pack I had hidden in an attic crawl space above my room. As he rifled through it, he found my picture ID. "Well, we have a name for this one" he pointed to me. "Put him in the cruiser" he said.

I was led off to a waiting patrol car and put in the back seat. At this point there were four police cruisers parked in front of the house, and for some reason I didn't yet comprehend - the fucking Hazmat team from the fire department was setting up, full body suits and all. As the sun began to set, the kids were still standing there cuffed in front of the garage door.

One of the cops and a fireman approached the cruiser and leaned in to my open window. "Look, off the record - can you help us?" I looked up surprised and said: "with what exactly?". He coughed uncomfortably and said: "look, we need to know what that contraption is in the garage. Is it a meth cooker, some other drug manufacture gear? I'll leave, and you can just tell the fireman here, but we need to know how dangerous it is". I almost choked laughing, then I said: "So that's what the HazMat team is here for? Ok, look....you let those two kids go and I'll tell you everything you want to know about the thing in the garage, and you don't even have to leave - I'll tell you both".

The cop went over and talked to a Sergeant, and both the kids were un-handcuffed and released. I saw the young lady look back at the cruiser with me in it with tears in her eyes as her companion led her away down the street. At least that turned out ok, the kids were out of immediate danger. I however was quite fucked. They would find my BOLO in the NCIC computer system, and I would spend many years and maybe as much as a decade in Federal Prison. The Underground Railroad had failed. I had failed. It would all be a forgotten foot-note in the annals of Anonymous failures. The cop returned with his fireman buddy: "ok, we let them go. Now tell us what that thing in the garage is". I really wish you could have seen both of their faces when I told them: "it's a beer making rig. It's just beer guys" I said through fits of the giggles.

After asking me about things like how much pressure it was under ("how much pressure is a can of beer under?"), and then the fireman lingering to get tips on how *he* could brew *his* own beer -

I was finally driven away and taken to the Richmond Police Station for booking.

Thursday - January 26, 2012 approx. 12:30 AM ET - Police Station - Richmond, CA - USA

I was actually just starting to drift off to sleep finally when the keys rattled in my cell door, and in walked the same cop who hours before had stuck a gun in my face and threatened to shoot me. He came in and leaned against the metal sink in the cell. Neither of us said anything for a moment. I stared at him while he stared at the floor. Finally he lifted his head and said in a quiet and sincere voice: "I want to apologize for earlier, at the house. I shoudn't have drawn my weapon on you, none of you were a threat to me. I knew you were protesters. Funny thing is, I actually support what you all are doing. But I had a job to do". I sat up on my bunk and thought about that for a moment and then said: "so why did you do it then?" I asked. He was surprised by the question, and then a bit embarrassed. He thought about it a long moment, and then in a voice almost inaudible it was so low he said: "This job sucks. You spend all day afraid for your life. I just want to go home at night to my wife and kid" he said slowly. Then he leaned forward to leave. "Anyway, I am sorry. I just signed the paperwork to drop the charges on all of you, you'll be processed out in a few hours". I sincerely doubted that, and I told him so. But he insisted I had been cleared for release. But I knew that if they ran me through NCIC which they had to do at some point, I was toast and going nowhere except straight back to the US Marshals in San Jose. So I went back to sleep.

Around 5:30 AM I was awoken by a black female jail guard. She pushed a small cardboard box through the slot on the bars. Inside was two pieces of soggy toast, two boiled eggs, the salt and pepper packets soaked and useless, and a milk carton that actually felt warmer than the frigid air temperature of the cell. "No thanks" I muttered and slid it back to her. I went to lay back down on my bunk as she said: "suit yourself sugar. I'll be back in a half hour to process you out" she said as she left. I muttered under my breath that I would believe it when I saw it and tried to go back to sleep.

Just after 6:00 AM my motherly matron in uniform came back, no doubt to give me the bad news and tell me to settle in. I was genuinely surprised when she opened up the cell door and said: "time to go partner" and gestured towards the hallway. Surely the US Marshals hadn't gotten here already, were they *really* going to *release* me from custody? This was honestly the first moment when I remembered the message I managed to get off in the final moments before the raid commenced. Could my hacker friend *really* have done it and eliminated my BOLO from the NCIC system long enough for me to slip through their fingers? If so, I may never know - but it would be the biggest fucking miracle that ever happened to me.

I was led out of the cell block in a daze. I simply couldn't believe this was actually about to happen. After changing back into my clothes and signing for my few belongings, I was led out to the front doors and I saw sunshine. My heart began to pound as I stood there hesitating to open the glass door and walk into the parking lot of the Police station. I scanned the cars parked there, were there any Crown Vics? Could this be a trap and the FBI jumps me when I walk out? I had heard numerous tales in the joint of just such things happening, I knew it was possible. What seemed quite *impossible* was that I had been caught and was still about to get away. I took a deep breath, and heart pounding I walked briskly out into the parking lot.

It was a bright and warm sunny California day. As I made my way briskly across the parking lot I was literally shaking I was so scared. I made it to the sidewalk, and looked back. No one was following me, no evil Crown Vic's made their appearance. I saw a large park up the street and made a b-line for it.

I needed to at least get my heart-rate down and smoke a cigarette. As I lay against the trunk of an oak tree and sucked hard on a crumpled cigarette I found in my pants pocket, I scanned the park and surrounding streets from relative seclusion. Birds chirped, people walked around in the sun with squalling little kids in tow. At the far end of the park a street person lay in the shade of another large tree sleeping soundly, insects buzzed....and absolutely *no* FBI or even other cops around.

    I sat there quite a while, probably almost an hour. Now what to do? I had *nothing* but the clothes on my back. Everything I owned was back at the safe-house. As insanely dangerous as it may seem, the only option seemed to be to make my way back there and see if any of my stuff was still there and try to make contact with any of the Underground Railroad folks. I asked directions from a passer-by and the house was many miles on the other side of Richmond. That figured. So....I walked. And walked. And walked. Up into the hill-side communities of the upper middle class.

    It took many hours, and the searing sun caused the temprature to soar. Finally in the late afternoon I staggered exausted and covered in sweat down the block where the safe-house was. Immediately I was accosted by the wonderful middle-aged lady who lived next door. She was so relieved to see me, she had yet to see anyone from the house return and she was worried the cops had done something to us. I informed her they dropped all charges and let us go, then tentatively I asked her if she saw them take anything from the house. She was adamant that she watched them like a hawk, and they took out nothing from the safe-house. I breathed a sigh of relief. I let her know I intended to break in, and she actually asked if she could come with me! "I'm worried about the chicken. I have two of my own, I'll keep her until the others come back if it's okay with you?" she asked tentatively. I was way ok with her taking the chicken, especially if my computer and backpack were still in that house.

I climbed over the side gate, and un-latched it from the other side and ushered the neighbor lady in. She immediately began the process of chasing down the chicken in the backyard while I went to see how lucky I really was today. We always left the kitchen window open and unlocked. Most of the time the screen was up also so the chicken could have free roam of the house. It was better at being a pet than at laying eggs, the latter of which it only did a few times a week - usually on the couch or someone's bed. Often we didn't get to eat these eggs, as the way in which they got discovered rendered that imposible. Humerous and messy, but impossible. But what if the cops in securing the building locked the kitchen window? Then I might have to actually break something to get in.

The window was closed, but a gentle nudge on the handle and it lifted right up. I rather gracelessly let myself in, climbing over a stinking kitchen sink filled with day old dirty dishes. I couldn't help but pause to put on a pot of coffee, something told me I was going to need it. Then with great trepidation, I went to my "room" and slowly pushed open the door. Other than my pack having been obviously searched and then un-ceremoniously dumped in the middle of the floor in dis-array, everything, including the computers - were exactly as I had left them. I looked around at the maps and Anon propaganda posters and memes taped to the walls and shook my head. What had these cops been thinking when they came into *this* room?

I quickly gathered up my gear and rolled it up for travel. Then I paused. It seemed safe enough, I decided to take a shower before I hit the road to....any where but here, I guessed. Just then the front door opened up with a bang, and Peter walked in with tears rolling down his face and looking around wildly like a mad man. He rushed up to me and pulled me into a fierce bear hug. I pulled away a bit confused, as he wiped tears from his face. "man, I thought for sure they had got you, the kids told me how you got them set loose and then they took you away.

I was sure we had failed you. How the fuck are you out?" he said visibly trembling. "I'll fill you in later, but right now it seems to me the thing to do is get my lucky ass as far from this place as possible" I said. "Agreed" Peter said, and without hesitation he started gathering up my pack and computer case and headed for the door.

We drove north, further up into the hills surrounding greater Oakland. Peter, for lack of a plan - was taking me to his parents house. They were in Europe for a vacation, and he had been ferrying Occupy people over there regular to clean up and rest. I'd be safe there while he contacted the "Operator" i.e. OpNoPro for instructions. For myself I didn't worry. I knew the general idea of the network we had created, and I just assumed the next "node" in the Underground Railroad would be in Oregon. A few hours later I got quite a surprise when Peter sat down to brief a newly fed and showered "package".

He began to by explaining: "OpNoPro thinks we need to accelerate your exit from the country. He says the weather along the border area is still chilly, but mild enough you can make it across. They are onto you trying to get out, and he's afraid if this drags on too long they'll dragnet the Northwest Border region to prevent you leaving. Especially after slipping through their fingers like this. We are sending you via Greyhound to the final US 'node' in Seattle. You leave first thing in the morning." he finished. So, this was it. My days of living care free in safe-houses was coming to an end. Now it would be all on me and my physical stamina and planning to literally hike for days across the Northwest Frontier into Canada. Time to do a "Grizzly Adams" routine and leave my own country, probably forever. My mood was somber as I assented to the plan they had for the "package".

Friday - January 27, 2012 approx. 9:00 AM ET - "Undisclosed Secure Location" - Richmond, CA - USA

My pack and computer case were in the driveway next to the car, and I was saying my last tearful goodbyes to some of the kids from the safehouse who had come to see me off. As I hugged the young lady who had been with me at the end when the Richmond Police kicked in the door, I whispered in her ear: "say good bye to the chicken for me". She giggled and sniffled back tears at the same time and smiled at me. Then we got in Peter's car and began the long commute into Oakland.

As we approached Oakland on the freeway, Peter got a call on his cell phone. As I watched he grunted a bunch of times with a serious look on his face, then paused....said "ok" and terminated the call. Sliding the phone back into his wind-breaker he turned to me in the passenger seat and said gravely: "we may have a problem". As he drove he explained. That was the black kid Jimmy I had met from Occupy Oakland, the one who looked out for me while I was briefly hiding there. He was there now in Oscar Grant Plaza, and like fifteen or more Crown Vics full of FBI agents just surrounded Occupy Oakland.

Peter and I decided to park several long blocks away from the Greyhound station and approach it carefully via side-streets to scope it out. I left my stuff in the car in case we had to beat a hasty retreat. As we came within sight of the back of the Oakland Greyhound station, there were two Crown Victoria's and an FBI "party van" - an electronic surveillance vehicle parked there. "Fuck shit!" I said under my breath as I smoothly pulled my hoodie over my head and turned on heel back to the car. Peter followed and we got in and drove away. "Don't worry, I have a plan" Peter said as he eased us back into downtown Oakland traffic.

Peter's plan was to activate a secondary resource he had in Oakland. A small network of safe-houses used by high-profile Occupy Oakland activists when they were being specifically targeted by the OPD. Most of these safe-houses were designed to be very temporary, a few hours to a few days at most.

But he only needed to keep his "package" safe until tomorrow, when the new plan was to drive me hundreds of miles north out of the city and its dragnet, and from there take the Greyhound on to my destination.

Saturday - January 28, 2012 approx. 11:30 AM ET - Greyhound Station - Mendocino, CA - USA

That night, Peter stayed with me the entire time. As reports continued to come in of the FBI presence at Occupy Oakland, they were followed by more disturbing reports of individual activist's homes being raided. And *everyone* was being asked about Anonymous. Peter decided to move me every couple of hours until dawn when we would head north. I don't remember how many times I was moved. I know that the last time I was half asleep, and then I awoke in the backseat of the car driving north up the Pacific Coast Highway. We pulled out a few hours later at the Greyhound station in Mendocino.

As I unloaded my gear from the car, Peter came around and gave me my ticket. There was a hundred dollars in the ticket envelope. "One last thing, this directly from OpNoPro last night, let me see that cellular WiFi modem you've been using" he said. I shrugged and dug it out of my laptop case and handed it over. Peter gently removed the battery, and underneath he gently nudged out the sim card with his fingernail. He handed the modem, which was smaller than a pack of cigarettes - and the battery back to me. Looking around, he fished out a pair of needle nose pliers from the inside pocket of his jacket. From his pants pocket a pulled out a bic lighter, and proceeded to burn to a crisp the little sim card - tossing the charcoal remnants under the car.

Monday - January 30, 2012 approx. 12:30 PM ET - Starbucks - Seattle, WA - USA

This Starbucks perhaps wasn't the ideal place from which a wanted hacker should be contacting his control. It was right around the corner from a huge Federal law enforcement complex, which included among many things one of the regional DHS "fusion centers". The place was literally swarming with G-men and women, DHS ex-military looking types, you name it. OpNoPro went from already extremely angry with me to a place where I thought it likely he might actually explode, like physically. It was a little kept secret that OpNoPro was the oldest known Anon in Anonymous. No one knew exactly how old (I do but I'm not talking), but most in the know thought it was well north of sixty (it is).

OpNoPro was already pissed at me because instead of contacting him the moment I got off the bus, I made him worry horribly as I went dark and just bummed around Seattle for a couple of days, hanging out in parks - bars and coffee houses. I needed some time to....de-escalate, emotionally after the past few weeks in the Bay Area. It was a lot to go through, and a lot to digest and find my equilibrium again. I knew I needed to be centered because this was it, this is where it was down to just my intelligence, cunning, and physical stamina. It was soon to be, as they say - all on me.

As OpNoPro got himself under control he briefed me, but rather needlessly. While I didn't know all the details of every "node" in the Underground Railroad, I was familiar with what was pre-determined to be the last "node". That's because it was joking referred to as my "exit node", a play on the Tor network some readers might get. Anyway, being the last "node" it had to be top shelf. I knew that the safe-house was a very well appointed private residence north of the city, owned by a man who had got very rich from developing mobile game apps independently. He was 100% loyal to OpNoPro, though not an Anon. He was a part of OpNoPro's personal network of pro-geeks and hackers. He was also rich, and ready to provide haven, staging space, and all the resources I desired equipment-wise to get across the border.

He would even arrange to have me dropped off about thirty miles south of the Canadian border at the exact location he had already been briefed on.

Also here in Seattle it had been arranged that I would finally meet with the investigative journalist from CNN, Amber Lyon. The plan was to meet her at a hotel in downtown Seattle where I agreed to sit for some interviews for a couple of days (which dragged into four days), just prior to my exit from the country. I had already informed her that my team had nixed the idea that she might actually accompany me as I hike out and film *that* part. Something told me from talking to this woman online in the weeks leading up to when we finally met that she was someone who just didn't take no for an answer. The paradigm didn't even exist in her world view.

Saturday - February 4, 2012 approx. 10:30 AM ET - Undisclosed Hotel - Seattle, WA - USA

It had been a busy few days of making myself available for shooting with Ms. Lyon. We shot mostly in the room, as I answered endless questions sitting in a high back chair roasting my ass off in front of a fake propane gas fueled fire place. When I needed a break to stretch or eat, Amber would follow me around Seattle with the camera. It was a bit disconcerting, although over the years I have learned to tolerate it better. Today as she began winding down and the day approached for me to take my leave of her, she told me I could just work, do what ever I do - and she would film that and then I was done. Eager to both catch up on Anonymous stuff, as well as be done with this very long interview process and get on with what I had to do - I gladly assented to spend a few hours catching up with my comrades.

First I made a Skype call to Barrett Brown, to inform him of what I was about to try and do and to talk to him about *Anonymous Operation Bahrain*.

At this point I thought I'd throw Amber a bone and let her join in, as she had been in Bahrain and even been arrested covering the protests there. Both Barrett and she were delighted to meet each other, and I was humbled to watch these two geniuses I had introduced interact. Barrett had just launched his *Project PM*, a crowd sourced wiki style think tank and depository on knowledge, mostly hacked - about the emerging surveillance-industrial complex. Amber wanted Barrett to research a shady pr company called Quorvis, who had a penchant for polishing the public images of kings and despots all over the world. Not only did these freaks take millions from "king" Khalifa in Bahrain, but because of Amber's coverage in Bahrain they had targeted her for a smear campaign and even successfully suppressed her documentary on the Bahrain protests.

As the evening wore into night, I got a ping from a member of my crew. Seemed that elements of my crew in conjunction with elements of AntiSec and Op Iran - had infilterated the government run secure E-Mail servers of the Syrian Government and had begun download. Over seventy million messages would eventually be taken including President Assad and his wife's personal accounts, and given to WikiLeaks - where they still reside to this day. I called Amber over to film over my shoulder as I got the early news and told her: "mark this well, this is history". All in a day's work in Anonymous.

Finally it was late, and I had been drinking some beer that Amber had bought. I wanted to go get some sleep before the big day tomorrow when I would get dropped on foot south of the Canadian border. I had a long arduous hike across an international frontier. I was just feeling the buzz from the beer and pot when Amber hit me broadside. "You know I still want to come with you" she said quietly at last as I poured over yet one more time the satellite images of my escape route. I was trying to memorize every tree and crevass of the route I had chosen, even though I had most of this downloaded and I could access it briefly in the field as long as I conserved my laptop battery.

"You know that is not possible Amber, it's too dangerous. For either of us" I said in dismissal. She pressed me. I put it off on Daniel, a young man from the safe-house who was the driver who would be dropping me tomorrow night. Daniel was new to this, but enthusiastic. And as a coder for some of the most sensitive projects at Boeing, he was a huge asset to Anonymous and information activism. Daniel was *super* conservative with op sec, he would definitely say no. "Look Amber it's protocol, I am still the 'package' until the moment I roll out of that car thirty miles south of the border and start walking. That means it's their call not mine". "Fine" she said, just a little too easily.

A few minutes later, Daniel arrived - quite anxious to meet the famous Amber Lyon. He was actually there to go over the final drop off plan one final time with the sat images. I could see already, I was being ambushed. When Amber suggested we go down to the bar and celebrate after I briefed Daniel, I knew she was willing to cheat to get her way. After swilling Amber's free booze and glowing in her "fame" for two hours, Daniel simply said "oh sure, you can come" when she finally asked him near midnight. Then he staggered off into the night to take a cab home. Great, now I only had to hike across the frontier with a journalist in tow. Piece of cake.

Sunday - February 5, 2012 approx. 3:30 AM ET - Thirty Miles South Of The Canadian Border - State of Washington, USA

After pulling out in a rest area in the middle of the night to study the satellite images on a picnic table one last time, we finally pulled down a one way dirt road. We knew, or sincerely hoped - that at the end of the road there would be a gate surrounding a farm field with a farm house in the middle of it. There was room we believed for Daniel to smoothly turn around once he got to the gate. As he swung around there would be a series of mailboxes and a crude wooden bus stop shelter.

The plan called for Daniel to stop for just the briefest moment and Amber and I, packs already on - would roll out onto the ground behind the shelter as Daniel smoothly drove away.

The dirt road seemed to go on for quite a bit longer than it should have, and I was begining to worry that already our plan of using resources like Google Earth would fail us. But sure enough, the gate and field appeared and looked just like I thought they would. Daniel slowed, turned around - and muttered: "good luck" as Amber and I hit the ground low and rolled behind the bus shelter. Daniel drove away into the night and Amber and I lay there a moment taking in the fact that this was it. We hadn't really exerted ourselves, but I at least was breathless from the anticipation near the end of the long drive up to the farm. We tried to quiet our breathing and listen for any sound that we had been seen. We had chosen a Sunday morning under the assumption it held the greatest chances of the family who lived in the house being asleep. But farms had dogs, and dogs made a fuss fast.

After a good fifteen minutes went by, I gave Amber the signal and we both stood upright behind the shelter and adjusted our packs. The plan now called for a rare bit of running, at least on my part. Ms. Amber, apparently - ran marathons. We had to run diagonally through the field for almost five kilometers in full view of the house through a tilled field in order to reach a treeline on the other side. It was the only point in the entire journey that we were to be thus exposed until we were already in Canada. At least according to the plan. So if anything was going to go wrong, it had the highest chance of happening in the next ten minutes.

I peered around the bus shelter. I saw no dogs, and all the lights in the farm house appeared to be out. I looked over my shoulder at Amber, who was adjusting a GoPro camera on a head-mount. I guess the documentary stuff starts now! I turned and I fucking ran. Slipping easily around the gate I began running as fast as I could muster towards the waiting trees that seemed way further away than a mere five kilometers. Amber was careful to stay behind me, after all - this was my journey.

She was young and athletic, I was glad I didn't have to keep up with her! The furrows in the field were deep, and they were hard with the winter freeze still. It was tough going, and we were both scared. It was cold enough I could see my breath as I finally approached the treeline, scanning through the dark for what to expect. Amber was hot on my heels when all of a sudden the ground seemed to drop away and a few feet below was a small bank of a large drainage ditch and the bank was covered in a cordon of vicious looking thorns, apparent even in the dark. Without even thinking I hit the air, as did Amber. We sailed well over the thorns, but landed square in the middle of the drainage ditch which had a thin layer of ice on top of two feet of frigid filthy water. The up side is we were out of sight of the farm house.

We were soaked, and trapped - as thorns lined both sides of the very large irrigation ditch that ran along the edge of the field. Nothing we could do but carefully pick our way north walking in the drainage ditch, carefully slogging through the knee deep mucky water - and looking for a break on the treeward side. After almost an hour, we found one and climbed up weary and shivering from the water onto dry ground, trees and dry winter grass. We were a mess, but we should be able to stay concealed within the forest until we were at least a few kilometers inside of Canada, but that still meant a few days of wilderness hiking. What could go wrong?

As the first hints of light began to show in the eastern sky, we rolled out our wet bed rolls, and wrapped ourselves in silver "emergency blankets", covered ourselves with pine bows for added concealment and insulation, and collapsed into unconcsciousness - both of us physically and emotionally drained.

Monday - February 6, 2012 approx. 12:30 PM ET - Somewhere South Of The Canadian Border - State of Washington, USA

We had gotten a fairly late start, arising at around 8:30 AM. I quickly brewed us up two strong cups of coffee and we drank them as our stuff hung in the sunlight to hopefully dry out more. I smoked some weed and several cigarettes. I admit to feeling cocky, as it seemed from my weeks of pre-planning this was looking about what it seemed on the Google Earth and other image databases we had studied at length. I busted out and fired up my laptop, mostly just to see how it had fared the night before. Thankfully it had survived. By 10:30 AM we were heading north west according to directions I had memorized. My plan called for climbing the side of a ridgeline, and descending into a heavily forested mountain valley that ran all the way into Canada. It had no buildings or roads or evidence of the grid - and I was certain it was the perfect way out of the USA undetected.

By noon, I knew the one detail in all this that always exists, the one detail in an otherwise perfect plan that you always overlook. As I clung to a fifty year old elm growing straight up out of steep shingled stone scree, dangling fifty meters above the forest floor I said it out loud: "gradient" I muttered to Amber clinging to a nearly identical fifty year old elm about five meters below me. Her hair was disheveled, and she was sweating. The GoPro on her head was still filming. In a rare display of anger Amber looked up at me and said: "what the fuck are you talking about". I found a way to remove my pack and wedge it into the tree, and I fished out my smokes and lit one. Amber looked down at the long drop, but then reluctantly did the same - sans the smoke of course.

"Gradient" I said again as she settled into some sort of balance with her tree so that she could rest and eat a granola bar. She did turn off the camera though. "I checked and re-checked the elevations a million times. But I forgot to check how *fast* shit gets high. Gradient, in other words. And that's why we are stuck up here like treed cats." I smiled down at her. "So, we *are* going the right way?" she asked dubiously. "Not anymore. Clearly we can't go any further without special gear we don't have.

And if you haven't noticed, one of the reasons we are resting here is because even getting back down is looking a wee sketchy at this point" and I smiled again, hoping to win her back with my dashing charm and wit. It wasn't really working, she simply went from angry to concerned as she looked down and realized I was right.

After an hour of extremely careful "one foot at a time" climbing, and more than a little graceless falling - we arrived back at the bottom of what I now knew to be an impassable barrier of sloping rock and knarled trees. We were none the worse for wear, but we had wasted much of the day. We made a sort of picnic rest camp with blankets and I busted out the laptop. "So, you have a back up plan - right?" Amber asked as I brewed us some coffee and studied the computer screen. "You Anons always have a back-up plan, right?" she looked up at me this time actually expecting an answer to a question I was praying was rhetorical. "Yeah well, sort of. I never really thought the first route wouldn't work. But I did make some notes about an alternative. Come here, let me show you something" I motioned her to look at the screen. "See that?" and I pointed at a very faint line on the terrain map from a satellite. "What is it? I thought there was nothing out here, nothing but wilderness" she asked. I boosted the gain even further to magnify the image, and it began to pixilate.

"Almost nothing. My research indicates that is an old smuggling road, probably carved out of the forest during prohibition in the States. They used it to run whiskey down from Canada. But the last time anyone seriously used it was probably backpackers smuggling pot into the USA in the nineties. I doubt we'll see a soul, or that anyone even knows it's there anymore. I only found it by accident one night studying these things. It will cost us almost an extra day because of time lost and time to get there. But if we do find it, we can just stroll through the deep forest into Canada" and I swished my finger along the line until it passed over the demarcation for the Canadian border superimposed on the image and smiled. Finally for the first time that day, she smiled back. There was hope on all fronts.

Thursday - February 9, 2012 approx. 1:30 PM ET - Canadian Border - State of Washington, USA

We found the old smugglers' road, just where I thought it would be - and we followed it for a day and half of real easy going. We took our time, relatively confident we would make it across without further incident. Twice there were low flying helicopters, almost certainly border patrol, impossible to tell from which nation, the USA or Canada - that sent us scarmbling into the under-brush to hide. But most of the time we just strolled along Huckleberry Finn style. The weather cooperated and was crystal clear sunny and tolerably warm during the day, and managably cold at night.

    We snaked along the bottom of the ridgeline, on the other side of which many kilometers away was the valley I had originally wanted to traverse the border in. We were paralleling it at a lower elevation, and although we caught occasional glimpses, we were well out of sight and well above the massive farmlands that straddled the border. When we finally came to the border, the valley actually spilled out from around the ridgeline to meet our little smugglers' road - which abruptly ended in a nearly impassable huge ditch of thorn bushes twenty five meters across. On a hillside over looking us, about thirty meters away but a world away with the thorns - was a huge megalithic rock boulder ten meters high and roughly carved as a sphere. It was the oddest thing I had ever seen until Amber whispered: "it's the border". I'll be damned, so it *was* marked. The sat images were not high definition enough to have picked out details like this, but she was right.

    It took us nearly three hours to traverse that final thirty meters and reach that strangely carved megalith. We had to cut our way through the wall of thorns, and we both sustained a fair number of injuries - some quite bad.

But finally we made it to the strange boulder and I whipped out my laptop to compare the topgraphy. Still bleeding I whipped my head around at the terrain below, as we were at altitude. This was it! The big stupid looking creepy rock was the exact border. I walked around it a bunch of times giggling as Amber filmed my mirth. Then I grabbed a stick and carefully drew a line east to west on either side of the rock, which was settled next to a very wonderful copse of douglas firs. I wrote USA in the pine needles on one side of the line and CANADA on the other still laughing out loud.

Bear in mind this "rock" was a good ten meters high and across. We set our things down on the "Canada" side of the boulder, and set to patching ourselves up from first aid kits stowed in our packs. While there was several hours of daylight left, neither of us much cared to try and press on that day after the field of thorns. The boulder was in a secluded area, and there was no spore of any other campers. We made ourselves at home on the thick bed of douglas fir needles. We made dinner, and Amber asked me some questions on camera about what it felt like to have officially made it into political exile in Canada. As we went to turn in Amber got up and went to walk into the darkness beyond the boulder. I asked her where she was going. "Back to the USA" and she pointed at the line I had drawn earlier. I sat up in my sleeping bag rather urgently: "*why?*" I asked. She smiled and flashed a handful of napkins as she stepped around the boulder. "Oh" I muttered. "Good enough reason I suppose" and I rolled over to spend my first night in my new country.

Saturday - February 11, 2012 approx. 1:00 PM ET - "The Muffin Shop" - Abbotsford, British Columbia - CANADA

When Amber and I awoke the next morning, we headed north from the boulder and up into Canada, and found a dirt road where we expected to.

For the rest of the day we walked back rural roads, until late in the night - stopping only once under a railroad trestle to eat lunch. Finally we staggered exhausted into Abbotsford, a tiny town on the frontier with British Columbia late that night. Amber insisted on shooting me walking into this muffin shop, like all determined to go back to work now that I am here. In reality the shot was staged, and Amber took a cab back to the States while I went behind the mall to a forested area and got some much needed sleep.

That was yesterday, and today was my first full day in country alone - and out of the Underground Railroad and on my own. I must admit to feeling quite liberated. It had been a positively surreal journey and adventure, and I was never at all certain I would make it. Here in the relative safety of Canada, for the first time in many years I could breath just a bit easier. But seeing that Canadian flag flying over the local fire station this morning gave me more than a moment's pause. My god, I was really in a foreign country - seeking political refuge from persecution within my own. Within the *USA*! And as always, the ever present notion of a one way trip. There is no going home this time, probably ever.

I had only one real chore after clearing a rather devasted E-Mail inbox. I had pre-written a Press Release in case I made it, and I blasted that to the media now to let the world know exactly what I had done and why.

Anonymous Press Release - Commander X Escapes Into Exile

Saturday - February 11, 2012

The Anonymous and the PLF are delighted to announce that Commander X, aka Christopher Mark Doyon - has fled the jurisdiction of the USA and entered the relative safety of the nation of Canada.

Using the Underground Railroad and network of safe houses created after the launch of Operation Vendetta in January 2011 (following the initial FBI raids on Anonymous USA), Commander X was spirited to the Canadian border - where he hiked through the forest of the North West into Canada.

The PLF would like to thank our friends and allies in Anonymous and the Occupy USA movement for their invaluable assistance in creating this dissident escape network, and for the great care they took with the first person to utilize it to seek freedom from the tyranny of the USA. Every person along the way acted with great discretion and professionalism, and treated the "package" with deep honor, respect and concern.

The Anonymous and the PLF calls upon the government of the USA to come to its senses and cease the harassment, surveillance - and arrest of not only Anonymous, but ALL activists. We DEMAND that the USA drop all charges against the Anonymous 15 immediately and apologize for harassing these courageous human rights and information activists.

We DEMAND that President Obama immediately grant a full executive pardon to Bradley Manning, and order an end to the investigation of Julian Assange. As for Commander X, he will release a communique shortly detailing his own demands of the government of the USA.

Anonymous and the PLF call upon the government of Canada to NOT co-operate with the USA in apprehending Commander X, or any other Anons or PLF Members. Anonymous reminds Canada of its decades long and noble tradition of harboring American political dissidents during times of great tyranny in the USA.

Finally we call upon all Canadian participants in Anonymous and supporters of the PLF to lend any aid or assistance possible to Commander X.

SIGNED -- Anonymous & The PLF

Author's Note: And with that I began my very public political exile in Canada. The Underground Railroad was behind me. Eventually with OpNoPro and other Canadian Anons help, I would cobble together a network of safe-houses and find resources and support here in the "North" as Canadians like to call it. And while I was destined to have many fantastic adventures here as well, nothing will ever touch those heady days in the *Anonymous Underground Railroad*. Those weeks of excitement and danger, with so many brilliant and courageous people working with such daring and innovation to just one goal, to get *me* to safety here in Canada - *Operation Xport* will forever be etched into my memory as one of the most fantastic journeys of my life. And it succeeded!

I and the others crafted what we thought and what our research had shown was a genuine and top-rate refugee network dedicated to Anonymous. We had puzzled for months over everything from protocol to who would be the "nodes". And when it came time to put that bold venture to the test, it had passed with flying colors. Despite stiff odds, and a massive attempt by the FBI to intervene - everyone (including amazingly, myself) kept their cool and worked through it. In the final analysis I have to say that the *Anonymous Underground Railroad* was one of the greatest creations of modern activism, a truly remarkable achievment of grass-roots organizing at its finest. I am proud and honored to have been a part of its creation and its primary beneficiary.

I have been involved in a very few rare Anonymous Operations that were truly covert in nature. There have been others as remarkable or more so than *Operation Xport*. Once, as part of *Anonymous Operation Syria*, we sent a crew of backpackers with four-hundred pounds of medical supplies (and ten pounds of chocolate for the children) over the border into Syria on foot in the last days of the protests before it became total war. It was a drop in the bucket of course, mostly a symbolic way to shame the western powers who refused to do anything to help in Assad's slaughter of the protesters. We sent tech help from the west to the protesters in Bahrain as a covert part of *Anonymous Operation Bahrain*. So it does happen that Anonymous is capable of organizing and flawlessly executing covert actions like Op Xport. But never doubt that hackers are capable of very sophisticated levels of planning and execution when it comes to covert operations. The history of Anonymous is replete with tales of this sort of thing. Maybe more Anons will decide to write books, and more of these remarkable stories of Anonymous organization can come to light.

It is vital that Anonymous and all information activists become savvy at building the sorts of complex support networks like the *Anonymous Underground Railroad*. We must learn to take care of our own fallen comrades, or we will fail. This means everything from legal funds and court support, to assisting those Anons like myself who choose to fight by seeking asylum. Our enemies are well resourced and highly organized. We can't do much about our resources, but we can at least step up to the task of building complex and sometimes covert action networks.

The original *Anonymous Underground Railroad* talked about in this book no longer exists. Such networks require constant attention and curation in order to persist, and the one spoken of in *Behind The Mask* was only used once – by me. But there is nothing stopping Anons in the USA, or anywhere in the world for that matter – from constructing their own covert version of the Anonymous Underground Railroad.

TEN

Exile

"If it's a choice between being silenced, or becoming a man without a country....then I choose exile."
~~ Commander X

Tuesday - May 1, 2012 approx. 12:30 PM ET - Starbucks - Montreal, Quebec - CANADA

One of the things that I determined once I began to contemplate my new life up here in Canada was that I would do everything in my power to avoid targeting any government or corporation here in this country. It just seemed like the sensible thing, not to make waves and give the RCMP a reason to want to hunt me. As the Greyhound bus pulled into Montreal on this wonderful sunny Spring day, I was making a point of mentally reminding myself of this. That I needed to lay low, not get caught up in either street protests or online actions that involved Canadian politics. Because Montreal was quite possibly the Anarchist capital of North America. And these people lived to protest, and the government and police were as corrupt here as in Mexico City. I had a feeling it was going to be difficult to stay out of trouble in this magnificent old world city.

Up until now, it had been fairly easy to lay low here in my new adopted country. As I made my way east via a safe-house and Greyhound stations, I gave E-Mail interviews about my dramatic escape from the USA - and continued my work in various ongoing Anonymous Operations around the world. This is a sparsely populated country, with a handful of major cities and vast tracks of wilderness in between. The people up here are so much more at ease than in America, and I was in country for over two weeks before I even saw a single uniformed police officer. I don't think the average American realizes the severe level of the surveillance and militarized-police state that they endure everyday as the norm. Or how refreshing and liberating it is to be free of that control matrix.

So as I arrived here in Montreal I was feeling good, and determined to behave myself and stay out of trouble. As so often happens, that resolve lasted less than a day. I made my way from the Greyhound station to a Starbucks on Rue St. Catherine.

I was just settling in and working on some E-Mail when I saw a bunch of media wagons and tv trucks begin racing up to the park across the street and begin setting up. I could see people on the sidewalks rubber-necking up the street so I decided to go have a smoke and see what was up. As I gazed up the street and tried to make some sense out of what I was seeing, I heard what seemed like the sound of a sporting event of some kind. As I would later learn, Montreal protests are always *loud*. Suddenly I could see them, *tens of thousands of them* - coming right down Rue St. Catherine. It was a massive protest.

    I was delighted. I knew that Montreal was a politically radical city, and people here loved to march in the streets. But to have a massive protest come to me on my first afternoon in Montreal like this was a real treat. As the protest got closer I saw that my initial estimate of how many people there were may have been off by a factor of ten. It was easily one of the largest protests I had ever seen, with over a hundred thousand people stretched out from the downtown core of Montreal all the way up Rue St. Catherine for many kilometers. It was massive. Because of the language barrier, it was not immediately apparent to me why they were even protesting. Everyone was wearing tiny red felt squares about an inch square, attached to their clothing by a single brass saftey pin. It was clearly a symbol of their movement, whatever that was.

    As the march approached from one direction it became obvious that the police had other plans. The cops were busy setting up barricades, breaking out grenade launchers and non-lethal shotguns, and generally gearing up for a fight. But for the life of me I could not see why, as the protesters were being very peaceful. But apparently the pigs were determined to allow them no further up Rue St. Catherine. The line in the sand they had drawn was pretty much the same block my coffee house was on. I began to be concerned, and a little angry.

It seemed the police were gearing up to actually start some shit with these people, and that was going to get ugly fast as there were a *lot* of people in the street. As the march washed up against the police line, the usual Mexican stand-off ensued. This was clearly going to end badly.

That's when it hit me, just as I flicked my butt into the gutter and the first line of the protest washed up against the immovable police line in front of the cafe like the tide coming in. It was May 1st, "May Day". Every May 1st workers, Anarchists, Social Democrats - and other so called "Social Justice Warriors" marched in just about every city in the world. This was definitely going to get ugly. I stepped back into the Starbucks, and moved with a purpose. I first got out a non-networked smart phone, inserted the battery - and fired it up. It was too dangerous for me to stream, but if I captured interesting video I could strip the metatags out later and upload it. Then I fired up my laptop, but I didn't boot into Windows. Instead I attached a special bootable external drive that fired up my customized version of Kali Linux.

First, I fired up my TweetDeck and opened up a browser. I wanted desperately to make sense of the little red squares of felt everyone was wearing, actually. My curiosity at that strange cultural iconography was killing me. What could it mean? And if there were so many of these folks protesting, and apparently it had been going on since way before I arrived - then why had the rest of the world not heard about what was essentially a street revolution in Montreal? As the Internet began to give me the answers I sought, the manager of the cafe came running out and locked us all in the coffee house as the Montreal police prepared to unleash hell on earth meters away in the street. And I sat there just watching it all unfold, my first few hours in Montreal - and I found myself in the midst of an insurrection with my laptop open and ready to pitch in. So much for my resolve to lay low and stay out of trouble here in Canada.

And then it happened.

With no warning or provocation, the frontline of the riot police let loose a volley of flashbang grenades, a tactic I had not seen since Oakland. One business man demanded the manager let him out so he could leave and get home. The manager tried to warn him, mostly in French - but he insisted. The manager shrugged, quickly twisted the bolt to let him slip out, then quickly relocked the door and watched. This well heeled dude in his expensive suit, trench coat, and leather shoes - he didn't even have time to turn around towards the street before a huge riot cop spun on heel and simply blasted him in the head with a huge wooden truncheon. As the manager released the lock, the poor fellow fell back into the Starbucks bleeding. To his enormous credit, the manager decided to forego the "I told you so" and went to get the first aid kit.

This was fucking madness. These cops were feral, and for no reason. Attack unarmed people in their own streets for what? For throwing a plastic water bottle that bounces harmlessly off your military grade body armor? For fucking real? Yeah....not on my fucking watch you pigs. I didn't dare get involved in a deep analysis of the Montreal Police department's servers while locked in a Starbucks in the midst of a full blown street battle, but a quick topical examination showed that it was a *really* old and mostly unpatched Apache web server. This meant that in all likelihood it was susceptible to a little known cyber weapon called a "Slowloris". Slowloris was a cool attack because if you setup the cannon right, a single individual could often take out an entire array of web servers single handedly. And often times these servers would stay down, even after the attack was over. Sometimes even for days!

I fired up the Slowloris script, entered the IP addresses and ports I wanted "lorised", and then set to capturing video and pictures with the smartphone through the Starbucks windows. Slowloris was powerful, but it would need about ten to fifteen minutes to build up enough strength to bring down the Montreal Police server array.

When I sat back down with a fresh latte, the Montreal Police web presence was a smoking crater in cyber space. I busted open Twitter to make the announcement and froze....how would I attribute the attack? As Anonymous Quebec? Anonymous Canada? Just plain old Anonymous? I knew from my brief research there was an Anonymous Canada and an Anonymous Quebec. But would they welcome my intervention in their "territory"? Finally I settled on the latter, and asked the owner of a generic Anonymous news account to put it out there and set it to going viral. I did however create a new hashtag which became almost emblematic of these protests going forward: #OpQuebec was born! By the next morning, the headlines in this city were all about a cyber attack I launched myself sitting in a Starbucks for the sole reason that I was pissed.

Tuesday - May 15, 2012 approx. 1:00 PM ET - Starbucks - Montreal, Quebec - CANADA

Just after I arrived in Montreal, and much to my consternation as I was trying to lay low - a reporter by the name of Catherine Solyom with the Montreal Gazette newspaper published a *huge* general profile piece on Anonymous. It was a Sunday edition, and it lead from the top three quarters of the front page itself with the Anonymous logo emblazoned across two thirds of the cover below the fold. It consisted of four more full pages inside.

It was insanely cool, well researched - and did focus on the seemingly huge impact that Anonymous was suddenly having not only globally, but right here in Montreal. I did something I have rarely ever done, and had only done once before (with Amber Lyon after her *Inside Anonymous* piece) - and I unilaterally reached out to a journalist. I wrote Ms. Solyom via E-Mail.

I complimented her on her piece, and told her that if she had run across me in her research and found me intriguing - that I might be nearby to provide access for an interview. I attached a copy of the press release announcing I had escaped the USA into Canada, and my PGP key for encrypting further communications should she desire.

She desired, she wrote back almost immediately and said yes she would very much like the opportunity to meet me in person and profile me in the Montreal Gazette. Hmmmm....didn't I recall some major resolution to not get all hot while I was up here in Canada, you know - lay low? Yep well that was well and truly gone out the window already. She was local, so the interview was not as difficult to arrange as some are, especially when bringing a journalist in from the USA. We bounced a few encrypted E-Mails and then arranged to have her and a videographer meet on the side of Mount Royale, a literal forested mountain with a giant lit cross on the top in the center of Montreal, and from which said city takes its name. The day had arrived, and the plan called for them to slowly ascend Mount Royale using a foot path. They would find me along the way up.

In fact I was perched above them with a tiny but powerful pair of binoculars watching from the moment they parked their car and got out their gear at the foot of the mountain. By the time they came upon me sitting on a rock, smoking a cigarette, and with a Guy Fawkes Mask laying in the sun-lit grass, I was quite certain they had not been followed. In a beautiful grassy sunlit and very secluded area on the side of Mount Royal in Montreal, Canada I proceeded to give this Catherine Solyom an interview that put her career over the top.

Catherine Solyom: As strictly an online army of hackers, how powerful is Anonymous?

Commander X: Anonymous is kind of like the big buff kid in school who had really bad self-esteem then all of a sudden one day he punched someone in the face and went,

"Holy shit I'm really strong!" Scientology (one of Anonymous's first targets) was the punch in the face where Anonymous began to realize how incredibly powerful they are. There's a really good argument at this point that we might well be the most powerful organization on Earth. The entire world right now is run by information. Our entire world is being controlled and operated by tiny invisible 1s and 0s that are flashing through the air and flashing through the wires around us. So if that's what controls our world, ask yourself who controls the 1s and the 0s? It's the geeks and computer hackers of the world.'

Catherine Solyom: What does it mean to be a leader of a leaderless organization?

Commander X: We don't sit around and elect a president but that doesn't mean there aren't leaders within Anonymous. Naturally Commander X or Barrett Brown or Peter Fein, whether they have names or are still anonymous, they take a leadership role and are looked up to. The average Anon is not like me, working 12 hours a day dedicating their life to this. He's an IT guy or a cable installer with a few hours to spare and he wants to be told what to do. It takes organizers to get things done. Anyone in Anon can be a spokesperson but my ability to speak is based on how much what I say squares with the consensus of the collective.

Catherine Solyom: It seems like there's a war going on between hacktivists or information activists and law enforcement. (At least 40 alleged members of Anonymous have been arrested around the world in the last year.) Who do you think is winning right now?

Commander X: I think it's a stalemate at the moment. I think eventually we'll win. I've always believed that right will always prevail. But at the moment the arrests have had a chilling effect on the movement.

For a 30-minute online protest I'm facing 15 years in a penitentiary. For the moment that's the only indictment against me but I expect there will be more. And it's not just about the potential penalty but it's the trial itself for which they delivered a terabyte of discovery. That's about 150,000 pages for a 30-minute protest. That means my trial will be two years long and during that time I'm under strict surveillance by the FBI. I can't access Twitter, Facebook or IRCs (Internet Relay Chats)– I can't contact any known member of Anonymous – who are about 50,000 people around the world.

So basically it shuts me down as an activist. Even if I prevail in court, I'm still shut down for three years. Well, I'm unwilling to do that – and that's why I'm Canada. In Syria and Tunisia, Libya, Egypt in Nigeria in the Ivory Coast, we have saved so many lives I can't even count – activists and journalists and bloggers and people who come to us to keep themselves safe in these extremely hostile environments – and I'm unwilling to lay that kind of work down.

Catherine Solyom: Now that you're in Canada for the foreseeable future, do you feel relatively safe?

Commander X: Yes. We have a lot of contacts in the Canadian government. We were well prepared when I came here, we have an underground railway, and safe houses in Canada. We might be wrong, but our understanding is that the Canadian government is about equally concerned with Anonymous and the United States. Their approach will be: "Step lively, don't stay long, and you'll be fine." So we're in negotiation with several countries in Europe to try to get a permanent political asylum situation set up for myself as well as for any other Anons and information activists who might need it. ... It's too bad Canada will not find the political courage to protect information activists from America like they did in the '60s with the draft dodgers.

That's the reality of it, but they will probably not actively seek to track me down.

Catherine Solyom: Do you think the general public is not concerned enough with online surveillance or real-life surveillance?

Commander X: I think the general public is beginning to learn the value of information. To give an example, for a very long time nobody in the U.S. or the world was allowed to know the number of civilian casualties in Afghanistan or Iraq. There were wild guesses and they were all over the ballpark figures, until a young army private named Bradley Manning had the courage to steal that information from the U.S. government and release it. Now we know that despite their smart munitions and all their high-technology they have somehow managed to accidentally kill 150,000 civilians in two countries....

As these kinds of startling facts come out, the public will begin to realize the value of the information and they will realize that the activists are risking everything for that information to be public.

Catherine Solyom: What do you say to people who believe Anons are just cyber-terrorists?

Commander X: Basically I decline the semantic argument. If you want to call me a terrorist, I have no problem with that. But I would ask you, "Who is it that's terrified?" If it's the bad guys who are terrified, I'm really super OK with that. If it's the average person, the people out in the world we are trying to help who are scared of us, I'd ask them to educate themselves, to do some research on what it is we do and lose that fear. We're fighting for the people, we are fighting, as Occupy likes to say, for the 99%.

It's the 1% people who are wrecking our planet who should be quite terrified. If to them we are terrorists, then they probably got that right.

"Information terrorist" – what a funny concept. That you could terrorize someone with information. But who's terrorized? Is it the common people reading the newspaper and learning what their government is doing in their name? They're not terrorized – they're perfectly satisfied with that situation. It's the people trying to hide these secrets, who are trying to hide these crimes. The funny thing is every email database that I've ever been a part of stealing, from Pres. Assad to Stratfor security, every email database, every single one has had crimes in it. Not one time that I've broken into a corporation or a government, and found their emails and thought, "Oh my God, these people are perfectly innocent people, I made a mistake."

Catherine Solyom: What do you think of the student protests in Quebec?

Commander X: Wherever I go, especially in the last two years, I have found protests. I had no idea this was going on in Canada and the day I arrived in Montreal I was in a coffee house downtown on the corner of Ste. Catherine and St. Hubert. And there was a protest right there at that park across the street. The entire intersection became inflamed, I watched police absolutely brutalize these kids, spraying can after can of tear gas, launching off pop-bang grenades, tear gas grenades, and the worse thing I saw these kids do, one of them threw a snowball, and one of them threw an orange rubber cone at these cops. I mean these cops are in full body armour for God's sake, that's not violence. But what was done to these kids was so violent that the coffee shop manager locked us all into the coffee shop. Locked the doors while all around us, literally in these glass windows all around us, we watched the kids get beaten down. Wherever I go whether Oakland, San Francisco, Montreal, everywhere I go I see the same stuff.

I see people rising up demanding justice and these brutal, paramilitary police departments being used to crush them and sure, I get involved.

Catherine Solyom: Anonymous started out as online pranksters but has gotten a whole lot more serious in the last two years. What happened?

Commander X: I believe Egypt was really a turning point for us emotionally in Anonymous. Obviously there was always that sort of prankster edge to us. But people often ask me, "Why are you so mean nowadays?" It started in Egypt – when you work for days to set up live video feeds and the first thing you watch through those feeds is people killing your friends with machine guns – that becomes personal.

And then it's not just Egypt, it's Libya, Tunisia, over and over again these Freedom Ops are really what gave us a sort of take-no prisoners attitude. We get to know these people. It may not be the same as you and I sitting here, but when you Skype with people and spend hours and hours talking with them on IRC (Internet Relay Chat) and they share their hopes and their dreams with you for their country, their future, when they tell you how they're risking their lives so their children can have a better future in some far-off land, you bond with those people and they become your friends and family.

Catherine Solyom: What's next for Anonymous?

Commander X: Right now we have access to every classified database in the U.S. government. It's a matter of when we leak the contents of those databases, not if. You know how we got access? We didn't hack them. The access was given to us by the people who run the systems. The five-star general (and) the Secretary of Defence who sit in the cushy plush offices at the top of the Pentagon don't run anything anymore.

It's the pimply-faced kid in the basement who controls the whole game, and Bradley Manning proved that. The fact he had the 250,000 cables that were released effectively cut the power of the U.S. State Department in half. The Afghan war diaries and the Iran war diaries effectively cut the political clout of the U.S. Department of Defence in half. All because of one guy who had enough balls to slip a CD in an envelope and mail it to somebody.

Now people are leaking to Anonymous and they're not coming to us with this document or that document or a CD, they're coming to us with keys to the kingdom, they're giving us the passwords and usernames to whole secure databases that we now have free reign over. …

Sunday - May 20, 2012 approx. 1:00 PM ET - Starbucks - Montreal, Quebec - CANADA

What began with my temper tantrum that first day in Montreal had now morphed into a full blown global Freedom Operation on behalf of the protesters called *Op Quebec*. By now I had liasoned with some francophones and we had put out a series of bilingual videos and press releases and other communiques. On this day, when the Montreal Gazette was running Catherine Solyom's profile piece on me - I was busy sucking lattes and hacking the Montreal Police servers every which way from Sunday. They were so insecure I had taken to just scanning the vulnerabilities and handing them off with script advice to other and sometimes local hackers working with the Op. We had already taken the website down more or less semi-permanently by deleting all the http files as well as their pathetic backup copy. In addition we had taken a slew of internal documents, some quite sensitive - and all their E-Mails. It was a colossal and brutal series of hacks.

But the poor battered Montreal Police were going to get a small break today, as our wrath was focused squarely on a pompous rich misogynist prick by the name of Bernie Ecclestone. Ecclestone owned the F1 circuit races. He had recently come into our sights in *Anonymous Operation Bahrain* when he ran a race there with the King's family as major investors despite the regime's horrific human rights record and the fact that the Kingdom was roiling with massive protests. Just after the city of Montreal passed their internationally denounced anti-protest bill "Law 78" to try and stifle the daily rolling marches that were paralyzing the city core, it was announced that Bernie's little circus was coming to Montreal. Just weeks after wrecking his sorry ass in Bahrain, we prepared to do it again in Canada. In a strange twist, hackers with Anonymous Bahrain would be joining me and hackers from Anonymous Canada in targeting the F1 servers.

We had even coordinated closely with a local Black Bloc of Anarchists on the ground in Montreal. They would launch a ground action, such as setting tires on fire at the main entrance to the race, and we would at that moment take out some part of the F1 online infrastructure or dump some part of it already stolen by us. The one two punches left the media salivating for more, and the F1 people positively on the ropes. A huge gala to launch the race festivities here in Montreal with lots of famous and powerful people was canceled at the last minute. All I could do was pray that this sudden uptick in Anonymous activity north of the border at the same time a famous Anon announced his escape here would not be noticed!

Sunday - August 12, 2012 approx. 12:30 PM ET - McDonalds - Toronto, Ontario - CANADA

Barrett Brown had left behind his active role in Anonymous to pursue his *Project PM* think-tank on the surveillance-industrial complex. He still wrote many articles on Anonymous activities, his old contacts serving him well at this point. We still stayed in contact, speaking several times a week as I briefed him on those Anonymous actions I was familiar with and working on. Today was a big day for him, because together with WikiLeaks he was revealing to the world an enormous and psycho piece of survelance technology called *TrapWire*. He had pinged me, and he and I had collaborated (one final time, as history would soon prove) on an *Anonymous Operation TrapWire*.

TrapWire quite simply scanned all public info on the Internet including everything from social media to IP connected CCTV cameras, even privately owned ones. But that wasn't to my mind the scary part. TrapWire then used an artificial intelligence to analyze this data, and the software itself could contact anyone from intelligence spooks to law enforcement if "it" sensed something "suspicious" in this mountain of data. It could then present its "findings" to a human in an easy to follow GUI for action. It was "Minority Report" level frightening crazy ass Big Brother shit at its maddest. Its revelation caused a massive and historic DdoS attack on both WikiLeaks and Project PM websites. And it ultimately hung a target on Barrett's back bigger than he could sustain, costing him his freedom at last. I was just finishing the E-Mail blast to hundreds of journalists of the Anonymous Press Release that Barrett, myself, and a couple of other Anons had drafted the day before.

Anonymous Operation TrapWire - Press Release

Sunday - August 12, 2012 11:00 AM ET USA

Greetings Citizens of the United States of America --

This weekend, it was disclosed by WikiLeaks the details about a system known as "TrapWire" that uses facial recognition and other techniques including high-end artificial intelligence to track and monitor individuals using countless different closed-circuit cameras operated by cities and other institutions, including private businesses. This program also monitors all social media on the internet.

The software is billed as a method by which to prevent terrorism, but can of course also be used to provide unprecedented surveillance and data-mining capabilities to governments and corporations - including many with a history of using new technologies to violate the rights of citizens. TrapWire is already used in New York, Los Angeles, Las Vegas, Texas, DC, London, and other locales around the USA.

The ex-CIA agents who help run the firm are old friends of Stratfor vice president Fred Burton, whom they've briefed on their own capabilities in e-mails obtained by Anonymous hackers and provided to WikiLeaks. Stratfor has engaged in several surveillance operations against activists, such as those advocating for victims of the Bhopal disaster - on behalf of large U.S. corporatons; Burton himself was revealed to have advocated "bankrupting" and "ruining the life" of activists like Julian Assange in e-mails to other friends. TrapWire is extremely expensive to maintain, and is usually done so at taxpayer expense; Los Angeles county alone has spent over $1.4 million dollars on the software's use in a single three-month period of 2007.

Although most of the regions in which TrapWire operates don't share information with each other, all of this is set to change; as Abraxas Applications president Dan Botsch told Burton via e-mail, "I think over time the different networks will begin to unite," noting that several networks had already begun discussions on merging their information.

Abraxas itself has always had the ability to "cross-network matches" from every region at their own office. By June 2011, Washington D.C. police were engaged in a pilot project under the Department of Homeland Security that's likely to lead to more cities using TrapWire on a more integrated basis.

Abraxas, the firm whose spin-off Abraxas Applications developed TrapWire in 2007, has long been involved in a lesser-known practice known as persona management, which involves the use of fake online "people" to gather intelligence and/or disseminate disinformation. The firm Ntrepid, created by Abraxas owner Cubic Corporation, won a 2010 CENTCOM contract to provide such capabilities for use in foreign countries; several board members of Ntrepid also sit on Abraxas.

The more we learn about TrapWire and similar systems, it becomes absolutely clear that we must at all costs shut this system down and render it useless. A giant AI electronic brain able to monitor us through a combination of access to all the CCTV cameras as well as all the online social media feeds is monstrous and Orwellian in its implications and possibilities. The Peoples Liberation Front and Anonymous will now put forth a call to arms, and initiate the doom of this evil and misbegotten program. We will use the following tactics to accomplish this goal:

1)   Anonymous will work closely with WikiLeaks and Project PM to gather, collate, disclose and disseminate as much information as possible about TrapWire and its related technologies and programs. This was begun this weekend, and already much has been learned. And they are scared of this, already many sites and repositories of data on TrapWire are disappearing - being taken down by those who do not want you to know the truth about what they are doing.

And WikiLeaks is at the time of writing enduring a massive and historic DdoS attack in an attempt to conceal this information from the public. We will do this not only to educate the general public regarding TrapWire, but to move them to pressure their representatives to shut down funding for this and similar programs of massive surveillance, and to pass laws outlawing the creation of future projects of this type.

2) ACTION ALERT - "Smash A Cam Saturday": TrapWire has access to virtually all CCTV's that have IP/internet connectivity. We have prepared an initial map/database of these cameras across the USA, and we will continue to expand this knowledge base.

   http://bit.ly/PcByYJ

While this database is a good guide to high priority camera targets, we encourage everyone to target any camera with IP/internet connectivity. We are asking everyone to sabotage at least one CCTV per week on what we are calling "Smash A Cam Saturday". We have provided this excellent manual of different tactics and strategies for disabling or destroying these "eyes of the beast".

   http://bit.ly/1Qjp

3)   As stated above, this "monster" doesn't just have eyes that need gouging out - it also has "ears". TrapWire constantly monitors social media. In a strange twist of fate, the company that developed TrapWire also works on something called "sock-puppet" programs. These are projects designed to create thousands of fake personas on social media. We will turn this idea and software against them, creating thousands of phony accounts and use them to produce a deluge of false triggers for the TrapWire program - essentially drowning it in "white noise".

4) Finally, Anonymous will do what we do best. We will find, hack - and destroy the servers where the AI "electronic brain" of this program is housed.

Operation TrapWire is a direct action of the over-arching Anonymous Operation USA. TrapWire is but one instance of how the government of the USA has turned against its own citizens, designating them as suspects and enemies. Now those citizens rise, and take back their country and their freedom. Welcome to the Second American Revolution.

We Are Anonymous

We Are Legion

We Never Forgive

We Never Forget

Government of the USA, it's too late to EXPECT US.

Press Release - http://bit.ly/OT3mNS

Additional Information - http://publicintelligence.net/unravelling-trapwire/

http://wiki.echelon2.org/wiki/Cubic_Corporation#Abraxas.2FAnonymizer

Anonymous Global - www.AnonymousGlobal.org

Wednesday - September 12, 2012 approx. 10:30 PM ET - Starbucks - Toronto, Ontario - CANADA

One thing it is important to realize about Barrett Brown is that he is sort of like the "Hunter S. Thompson of the Internet". He sees himself that way, and has successfully cultivated his online persona to such an extent that the world had come to see him that way as well. Lately, Barrett had been holding court late at night on a video chat platform called *TinyChat*. He had even given a major video press conference while in a bubble bath sipping a glass of wine. That was Barrett, and I loved him. Tonight again found him holding court in the video chatroom with around a dozen others, drunk off his ass and high as a kite - and half-naked.

   I often visited him there, but it raised such a fuss when I did so as *Commander X* that tonight I had snuck in to the chat channel with no video feed and under a false screen name. When it happened it was completely unexpected and with blinding speed, and it unfolded for all the world to hear and watch. In fact several people in the chat that night were recording and you can still watch it on YouTube. Suddenly you heard Barrett's front door splinter in with a crash, and his girlfriend did him the dignity of gently closing his laptop lid thus hiding from the world the moment when the FBI flung a screaming Barrett Brown to his carpet. Live on the Internet Barrett Brown, one time spokesman for Anonymous, national security researcher, world reknown journalist, and the Internet's favorite fool - had been arrested by the FBI....

Sunday - November 4, 2012 approx. 8:30 AM ET - Starbucks - Toronto, Ontario - CANADA

My morning started out strange and sad. As I went through my morning "chores", checking news feeds and clearing my E-Mail inbox - one message caught my eye. It was from an unknown address and contained only a link to what's known as a "burner note", an encrypted password protected online message that vaporized once the link had been clicked and the note read.

A few weeks after I successfully crossed the border, I had sent Absolem an encrypted message letting him know that the *Anonymous Underground Railroad* stood ready to help him escape the persecution in the USA as well, and that I would gladly share with him the support network that I was slowly building for myself here in Canada. I clicked the burner link to read his reply, which moved me to tears.

Dear X --

First I want to tell you that I miss you and I wish I could talk to you more. I have so many questions about life and how to be free from all of this crap without worry. I'm not leaving, at least not yet. I just wish I felt like my sacrifice meant something. I'm not looking for credit just an understanding that I'm there, I guess. Very few know me for what has happened and most ignore me for whatever reason. Also my living situation is no bueno. I've yet to meet a person that knows anything about Anonymous or Wikileaks, not to mention the complete lack of computer knowledge. You point any of these ppl away from facebook and they get scared. Anyway, I'm sorry I won't be able to join you just yet. As much as this sucks I need to go through it. I won't leave the others. I have no problem that you left as it's a completely separate matter and I feel better knowing you're out there :)

Plus your 10x more badass on the road than you would be chillin somewhere, Lulz :)

TL;DR I love you. I'm not coming. Be safe. Tell the Tunisian ppl to keep their heads up and that I said hi! :)

Commander Absolem

p.s ^^ I like that better :D hahaha

Next on my agenda was something that I must admit was a bit exciting. I had been contacted by an Editor at Rolling Stone Magazine. She was doing a piece focusing on Anonymous and Jeremy Hammond. I was meeting her in IRC chat to do a pre-interview interview. We had already agreed that she was coming to Canada the next day to talk to me in person, and to receive a secret stash of intelligence we had gathered on the famous Anonymous turn-coat "Sabu" who had recently flipped and started working for the FBI. I refused to send the sensitive info to her across the net, and so she agreed to meet me in Toronto.

Janet Reitman: Hello. would you be able to answer some questions for me, off the record for now if you'd prefer, on Sabu and/or Jeremy Hammond, and/or the political evolution of Anon? - I'm doing a very big story on the busts of the Lulzsec/Antisec guys, and am looking one, for info/insight about them, and two, for info about the culture of "hacktivism" as done by Anon.

Commander X: Well well, am I FINALLY going to be on the cover of the Rolling Stones? Lulz. I just ordered breakfast, please be patient with my reply time. And if you are patient with me your interview may be on the record, I have no problem with that.

Janet Reitman: So, I gather you're in a bit of trouble, and living in Canada for the moment...

Commander X: Hehe, ya think? Yeah they call it a....Federal Grand Jury Indictment yeah yeah dats it.

Janet Reitman: Oh yes, those. Sigh. How old are you, mind me asking?

Commander X: I am 47. So, on the Santa Cruz assault. Which is by the way a lousy 30 minute take down, carefully timed and executed in the midst of the PayPal/MasterCard attacks - I face 15 years in prison and a quarter million dollar fine. Yes, uhmmm there's a FreeAnon wiki I leaked all my paper work to. You can read the indictment etc. Anyways....So, that attack happened in between MasterCard and PayPal - like Dec 19 2011 I think but you'll have to check. As for being "famous", Arron Barr is the one who made me famous. I still want to meet this poor fellow Ben DeVries someday.

Janet Reitman: Who is the head honcho do you think?

Commander X: Of Anonymous?

Janet Reitman: If there is one.

Commander X: Hahahahahahaahahahahaha. Always the first really dumb question of every interview.

Janet Reitman: I know that anon is allegedly "leaderless." I don't actually buy that, but I buy it up to a point. No actually that wasn't a dumb question b/c I am well aware that your answer would be there are no leaders and so on. I don't believe there is a head honcho.

I do believe there are people like yourself with significant influence/respect/what have you - opinion leaders.

Commander X: I do have a lot of power in the movement. You can see that by the difference people pay to me in Op Bahrain. But trust me this movement is like an 18 wheel truck carrening down the highway with no fucking driver at the wheel.

Janet Reitman: I get that. I am quite skeptical of the FBI's attempt at "domestic terror"-izing you guys. It's stupid. Nonetheless, they seem intent on doing it.

Commander X: Well. The term Terrorist denotes that someone is scared right?

Janet Reitman: Indeed.

Commander X: I think the government IS scared of us. Terrorized if you will. And frankly they should be.

Janet Reitman: Indeed! Tell me why?

Commander X: We wield ten times the power of the USA government. I don't argue with the term, if thats what they want to call us so be it. We are the most powerful group or movement on the planet. We wield ten times the power of the USA.

Janet Reitman: Not to be rude, but you gotta convince me of that. give me concrete reasons/examples why this is so. In other words, help me explain to my readers who you are.

Commander X: We will. Believe me as this year unfolds we will. But let me ask you this, who do YOU think invented "Occupy"?

Because I was THERE in the IRC when WE invented it. Of whole cloth. In JUNE of 2011. It originally sprang from an Op to end the fed. But we added to that what we learned in Egypt. Know what that was? It don't take 99%. It don't take even 1%. Dig this. 40,000 people took Tahir Sq. Held it. And toppled a dictator. One of the most powerful and entrenched tyrants in the world. We took him out in 18 days. By taking and holding...occupying, but one small part of the public commons. We are the Egyptians. We are the Tunisians. We are Anarchists and transnationalists. We are every freedom fighter in the world, one mighty fist of freedom.

Monday - November 5, 2012 approx. 8:30 AM ET - Bloor Theatre - Toronto, Ontario - CANADA

Fleeing the publicity surrounding the huge profile piece on me that had been published in Montreal, I jumped from the frying pan into the fire by coming straight to Toronto for the world premier of the full length documentary movie about Anonymous by Brian Knappenberger entitled *We Are Legion*. Brian and I had corresponded via encrypted E-Mail, and we had a rough plan for some fun laid out. It would be real edgy, and extremely dangerous - but Brian was game for the sake of the movie and so was I.

We Are Legion was much anticipated, I arrived at the world premier to play my part wearing my brown Guy Fawkes hoodie, my all access pass around my neck and a real Guy Fawkes Mask on my face. To complete the costume, I wore black glooves and sunglasses under the mask to hide even my eyeballs. I pulled up to the famous *Bloor Theatre* in a limosine with the Editor of Rolling Stone Magazine, whom I had invited at the last minute to come along. Brian had scrambled to find her tickets, and in an interesting and ironic twist -

she would *not* be sitting in the VIP section along with Biella Coleman, myself - and others. No, the Editor of Rolling Stone rated nose bleed seats in the balcony seating!

As we pulled in front of the theatre my mind was blown for the first of many times that night. The line for the show ran around the block and out of sight up a side street. And both sides of the street in front of the Bloor were lined with media trucks. There seemed like well over a thousand people were milling about, and Toronto police were actually having to deal with crowd control! And there surrounded by the flashing neon lights of the Bloor marquee *Tonight: We Are Legion*. Wow. I have to admit to feeling a bit like a rock star as I stepped from the limo and was swamped by people shouting look it's *Anonymous,* and asking me to sign their programs for the nights showing. Of course none of these people knew who I actually was, and I signed them as my role that night demanded - *Anonymous*.

Brian sent security out to gently but firmly escort me and my guest inside the theatre, as I was begining to create quite a stir on the sidewalk. As I was escorted through the lines and into the front foyer of the Bloor Theatre I saw Brian Knappenberger standing beside Gabriella Coleman. I gave Biella a quick hug, and then we were both led to the VIP section and marked seats.

I had the honor of sitting next to Biella for the show, but only because I changed the seating signs around myself while Brian wasn't looking. After the sort of unbearable waiting you endure at any anticipated movie on the big screen, the lights finally went down and the world premier of *We Are Legion* began. Here are some of the more memorable and epic quotes from scenes in the movie:

"Individual nameless, faceless folks are having geo-political impact. It's both exilerating to realize that, and terrifying to realize that. It kind of depends on how that power is wielded." ~~ Joshua Corman

"I would love to live in a country where the government fears its citizens, and not the other way around. But right now, plenty of Anonymous actors are in hiding because of fear of reprisals from their government." ~~ AnonyOps

"Anonymous and the people on the Internet stood up and said: 'go fuck yourself'. You want to turn off the Internet? Fine! The people on the Internet will show them how to turn it back on." ~~ Mercedes Haefer, aka "The_N0

"I don't want to compare myself to someone like Ghandi or Dr. King. But they were one person, and they were willing to go out and change the world - and their messages live on everyday, through everybody. To have a chance to do something like that and not take it is foolish." ~~ Josh Covelli, aka "Absolem"

"It's worse now for humans post 9/11, because intrusion and surveillance, which is always going to be misused by those who can misuse it - has created a different kind of society. Freedom to move unobserved is a privilege only of the rich. Privacy is a privilege only of the rich. Hackers see the technology as giving them sanction to buy that privileged exclusion as well. It's intrinsic to the technology, the power to self-transcend and get out of the hump of the bell curve and move forward to a par with the master's of society, and do battle with them on an equal and level playing field. That's hacktivism!" ~~ Richard Thieme

"I have stood upon the mountain called Anonymous, and looked down on a world enflamed with revolution." ~~ Commander X

I can not adequately describe how I felt as I exited the theatre that night, still in Mask - and walked with Biella and Brian to a private post-release reception that he had arranged. I remember the area in front of the theatre was still packed with people and media as I looked up at the neon ringed marquee one last time. To have lived what we had done in Anonymous was one thing. But to see it presented so dramatically on the big screen like that, it took my breath away. Anonymous had definitely reached a pinnacle.

I recall a sense of the purest wonder at the notion that a small ragtag band of online activists had started something four years ago that grew at a blinding speed into such a global phenomenon that they would make movies about it like *that*. I also recall spending most of the rest of that night at the reception, and for many days after - wondering what would come next? Now that we had achieved this Global Collective, and the power that came with it, and it had gone viral and could not be stopped - what would happen now? What sort of demon or demi-god had we unleashed upon the world?

And what about this titanic and collosal confrontation between Anonymous and the "Five-Eyes Nations" of the West and NATO? How could that possibly end well, unless we could somehow get them to back down? Did we have *that* much power? In all honesty I doubted it. And I won't lie, the prospect frightened me nearly to death. But my wildest nightmares could not have possibly prepared me for what would come in the years following this story. I had no clue as to the magnitude of the darkness that was slowly heading towards myself personally and Anonymous, like a churning hurricane of pure evil. We would stand and deliver, for the world and for each other. But many would fall, some would even be killed. Even more martyrs and heroes would be created. Anonymous *would* survive, but at what cost in human life and liberty?

....To Be Continued.

Authors Note: And so the tale of *Behind The Mask* is complete. I started writing this book just after the premier of *We Are Legion* portrayed in the final scene. It took me nearly three years to complete, and another year to prepare it for mass publication. I pray the reader found it both enjoyable as well as enlightening. I have never written a book before, and I had no idea how hard it really is. My hat tip to all my author friends, this job is not easy. In any case I did my best and all of the many mistakes I am certain will be discovered over time are completely my fault and I apologize in advance for them.

Shortly after the day of the world premier at the Bloor Theatre, Nate Anderson of Ars Technica magazine came to Toronto and I sat for many long hours being interviewed for a profile series in his publication. I consider it one of the best of this sort of piece that has been done on myself and Anonymous. And because so much of these profile articles paralleled the story in *Behind The Mask*, I decided to include a snippet.

Excerpt From "The First Anon In Exile" Published in Ars Technica & Written By Nate Anderson

"You scared?" asks the fugitive in the camouflage pants as he sidles up to our pre-arranged meeting point in a small Canadian park. He wears sunglasses to hide his eyes and a broad-brimmed hat to hide his face. He scans the park perimeter for police. "Cuz I'm scared enough for both of us."

It's a dramatic introduction, but Christopher "Commander X" Doyon leads a dramatic life these days. He jumped bail and fled the US after the FBI arrested him in 2011 for bringing down a county government website—the only Anonymous-affiliated activist yet to take such a step. When I meet him months after his flight, he remains jumpy about getting caught. But Doyon has a story he wants to tell, and after he removes his hat, sunglasses, and backpack, he soon warms to the telling of it.

It's the story of how, in Doyon's words, "the USA has become so tyrannical that a human rights/information activist would feel compelled to flee into exile and seek sanctuary in another country."

On December 16, 2010, at exactly 12:30pm, Doyon issued a typed order into an Internet Relay Chat (IRC) room used by the hacker collective Anonymous. "CEASE FIRE," it said in all caps. The command had no visible effect in the Starbucks where Doyon was working, though somewhere nearby the Web servers for Santa Cruz County, California groaned back to life after being flattened by a 30-minute distributed denial of service (DDoS) attack meant to protest an ordinance that regulated sleeping on public property.

Doyon unfocused his attention from his laptop screen and looked up at the coffee shop around him. Real life rushed back—the buzz of conversation, the smell of roasted beans. No one paid him any special attention, but Doyon felt a sudden pang of fear.

"It dawns on me… this isn't Paypal or MasterCard," he tells me when we meet in Canada. "This is fucking two blocks away. I just took down a government website two blocks away—and I told everybody I was going to do it. My heart starts to pound."

He stepped out of the coffee shop and onto Pacific Avenue. Down the street, a reporter from local TV station KSBW was doing a "stand-up" with the Santa Cruz chief of police, asking the chief about the just-concluded denial of service attack. The chief was looking right at him.

So Doyon hopped a bus that took him into the mountains 20 miles outside of Santa Cruz proper, where he hiked up to the "pot camp" he called home for the moment. He stayed in the camp for a full week, scared of pursuit, until he was eating crusts of bread. The winter weather turned cold and wet, and Doyon grew miserable and hungry

He returned from the mountains to his old haunts in town and eventually to his regular coffee shops—despite knowing this "was a bad fucking idea." He had reason to worry; over the last decade, by his own admission, he has done nothing but cause trouble in Santa Cruz. The cops knew him well.

One day in mid January, Doyon dropped by a favorite coffee shop, sat down, and opened his laptop. The barista was acting odd, giving a strange jerk of his head that made Doyon wonder if the man had a tic in his neck. Doyon logged into his password-protected computer and had just started work on the "operations" that take up most of his time when "a fucking arm comes from fucking behind me" and snatches his laptop by its screen. Doyon looked up to find a local cop holding his machine. The sudden realization of what happened hit him hard.

"I'm fucked," Doyon says, remembering the moment. "They got the computer running."

Doyon could be looking at years in prison. The thought of long-term confinement was intolerable. He decided to run. On screen, his documents were open for anyone to read: the press release announcing the attack, the Anonymous chat logs used to coordinate it, the High Orbit Ion Cannon (HOIC) computer attack tool. Out from the back room came a couple of FBI cybercrime agents in their "scruffy-ass fucking hoodies" and blue jeans. Doyon, one of the 40 Anons raided that day in a major sweep across the country, was served with a search warrant. In a press release announcing the raids, the FBI reminded people that "facilitating or conducting a DDoS attack is illegal."

Doyon wasn't immediately arrested on the DDoS charge, but he knew that a net was closing around him. He returned to his mountain camp and "smoked some fucking weed" before considering his options.

The feds had all the data they needed to tie him to the Santa Cruz County attack, and he knew that Federal charges were serious —"intentional damage to a protected computer" under the Computer Fraud and Abuse Act (CFAA) is punishable by up to 10 years in prison and a fine of $250,000.

"Conspiracy" to attack a protected computer could add another five years. All that Santa Cruz County would have to show was that Doyon had caused $5,000 in damage (in the end, the county came up with a figure of $6,300), and he could be looking at years in prison. For someone who had lived outdoors for years, the thought of long-term confinement was intolerable. Doyon decided to run.

Within 48 hours, he had stowed his belongings in his mountain pack, hiked down the ridgeline from his camp until he struck Route 1, and hitchhiked north to San Francisco. He "ran in circles around the Bay Area" for a few months, moving from Berkeley to San Francisco proper to Silicon Valley cities like Mountain View. Doyon claims that a source within the FBI's cybercrime division got in touch and warned him that a grand jury had issued an indictment and that an arrest was imminent.

Right around the begining of 2011, a number of us got together in an online collaborative writing forum generically called a "pad", and composed an open letter from Anonymous to the World. I think it would be informative to include it here in it's entirety.

A Message From Anonymous To The World:

Hello World - We are Anonymous. What you do or do not know about us is irrelevant.

We have decided to write to you, the media, and all citizens of the free world to inform you of our intentions, potential targets, and our ongoing, active campaign for the freedom of information exchange, freedom of expression, and free use of the Internet.

Our message is clear:

We support the free flow of information. Anonymous is actively campaigning for this goal everywhere in all forms. This necessitates the freedom of expression for: The Internet, for journalism and journalists, and citizens of the world. Though we recognize you may disagree, we believe that Anonymous is campaigning for you so that your voice may never be silenced.

The recent news of our campaigns has been, at best, misinformed. We are not a terrorist organization as governments, demagogues, and the media would have you believe. Rather, Anonymous is a spontaneous collective of people who share the common goal of protecting the free flow of information on the Internet. Our ranks are filled with people representative of many parts of the world and all political orientations. We can be anyone, anywhere, anytime. If you are in a public place right now, take a look over your shoulder: everyone you see has all the requirements to be an Anon. But do not fret, for you too have all the requirements to stand with those who fight for free information and accountability.

Accordingly, Anonymous is not always the same group of people: Anonymous is a living idea. Anonymous is an idea that can be edited, updated, remanded--changed on a whim. We are living consciousness. At this time, Anonymous is a consciousness focused on actively campaigning for the free flow of information and accountability by our public institutions. We ask the world to support us, not for our sake, but for your own. When governments and corporations control information they control you.

When governments are allowed the power of censorship, they are able to commit great atrocities and act in corrupt ways -- free from the scrutiny of those from whom their power derives. When corporations are capable of using their vast amounts of wealth to manipulate or influence the free flow of information, they control you.

We are taking a stand against this--we refuse to be deceived!

The Internet is one of the last bastions of the free flow of information in our evolving information society, and one that is capable of connecting us all. Through the Internet, all the people of the world have access to information. When we all have access to information, we are strong. When we are strong, we posses the power to do the impossible--to make a difference, to better our world. This is why the government is moving on Wikileaks. This is what they fear. They fear our power when we unite. Please, do not forget this.

Our intention is just:

The intention of Anonymous is to protect free flow of information of all types from the control of any individual, corporation, or government entity. We will do this until our proverbial, dying breath. We do this not only for our selves, but for the citizens of the world. We are people campaigning at this very moment for your freedom of information exchange, freedom of expression, and free use of the Internet. Please remember this as you watch the news, read posts on Twitter, comment on Youtube or Facebook, or send email to a friend or loved one: Anonymous is making every effort to defend free speech and free information on the Internet.

We ask for the attention of the world as the events that are unfolding are fundamentally influencing the course of history.

Anonymous' campaign will defend against any individual, organization, corporation, and/or government entity that seeks to hinder the free flow of information on the Internet and beyond. Our methods may appear to be unjustly burdening our targets, but we argue that in this moment when the Freedom of Speech is under attack by the very institutions which are supposed to support it, drastic measures must be taken. During the Civil Rights Movement in the 1960s, access to many businesses was blocked as a peaceful protest against segregation. Today much business is conducted on the Internet. We are using the LOIC to conduct distributed denial of service attacks against businesses that have aided in the censorship of any person. Our attacks do no damage to the computer hardware. We merely take up bandwidth and system resources like the seats at the Woolworth's lunch counter.

Please, do not despise us, as we are not the Anonymous that you may be familiar with. Anonymous' past is not our present. May we remind you that Anonymous is a dynamic entity. Furthermore, anything attributed, credited, or tagged to Anonymous is not always based on the consensus of us as a whole. Even the document you read now was written by at least ten people simultaneously. Anonymous' campaign does not intend to harm websites of the individual citizen, organization, or government, that supports the free flow of information. We are here for all of you; to campaign for all of you. Where others have made this promise and failed, we make this promise and aim to keep it for everyone. Anonymous wishes to defend the free flow of information on the Internet and beyond; We would like to ask that you as a citizen, organization, media organization, or government do the same. Any individual, organization, corporation,and/or government entity which supports Freedom of Speech and a free Internet is an ally of Anonymous.

Our method of choosing targets is simple:

We are against anyone who supports censorship, such as those who are responsible for the silencing of Wikileaks.

We are against any entity that work towards the defilement of free speech and/or the free flow of information.

Our request of you is simple.

We ask you to consider the value of your natural Freedoms.

We ask you to consider the value of free information for you and future generations.

We ask you to consider the implications of information censorship, be it through the Internet or physical speech.

We ask you to consider the future of your own human rights, as those who wish to take these rights from you now will not stop with this.

As I pen these final words of *Behind The Mask* it is five years since we released the above communique. It was eventually made into a simple video as well. My blog *Commander X Speaks: The World Through Sunglasses* that I created during this period has continued to gain in popularity. I have included two pieces I wrote on *Anonymous* sometime after this part of the story ends in Toronto:

The State Of Anonymous: A Decade Of Lulz And Revolution

November 5, 2015

As the Global Collective of Anonymous marks our 5th Annual Worldwide Million Mask March, I thought it might be useful to examine the current state of Anonymous. As I pen this article, an estimated 1.5 million Anons are marching in Mask on their seats of government in approximately 675 cities around the world.

"Remember, remember the 5th of November – the gunpowder treason and plot. I know of no reason the gunpowder treason should ever be forgot!"

To begin, let us examine the broad state of the Global Collective of Anonymous as it stands ten years out. We have currently identified some 85 National Cells of Anonymous worldwide, with approximately 2.5 million active participants. To be included in this list we looked for three primary criteria: a stylized and unique national logo, an active Twitter account – and a website of some sort. Now obviously, National Cells such as Anonymous Afghanistan or Anonymous Vietnam are quite likely very small – consisting of perhaps a few dedicated individuals in those countries. But others, especially in Africa (check out Anonymous Kenya) or South America (see the amazing Anonymous Venezuela) are some of the largest National Cells in our Global Collective – and are very active and effective politically within their country's sphere. And even more amazing is that many of these "third world" National Cells dwarf their western counterparts such as Anonymous USA or Anonymous UK.

In the past year we have seen some truly epic and historic Anonymous Operations conducted by these incredible National Cells of Anonymous working together or on their own. These Ops have truly had a magnificent impact politically and socially. From Operation Ferguson in the USA (www.OperationFerguson.cf) to Anonymous Honduras recent Operation No More Corruption that managed to bring down their government in about a month –

Anonymous is making it's might felt all across the world this year more powerfully than ever. In the past couple of years Anonymous Philippines has been so successful both online and in the streets that they have quite dramatically changed the political dynamic in that country, leaving their government in tatters and quite afraid of this enormously powerful National Cell. Anonymous Palestine, while it is a compact National Cell has not only been battering Israel over the Occupation – but they even had enough resources to spare that they were able to be extremely helpful to Anonymous Operation Ferguson in it's early weeks last year.

And in a strange twist, Anonymous Operation ISIS lead by the powerful allied crew Ghost Security has been more effective in the past year at denying these terrorists access to the Internet and social media than all the worlds intelligence and law enforcement agencies combined! An incredible feat for a small group of hacktivists with almost no funding.

No assessment of the current state of Anonymous would be complete without an examination of certain conflicts currently raging within or between a few of the National Cells. First a general word about conflict within Anonymous. It should not surprise anyone that in a massive global movement based at least in part on cyber warfare, that at some point a bit of in-fighting will break out. Not only is this inevitable, but it is sometimes good for the movement in the long-term as it serves as practice for when we turn our sights on the governments and corporations.

The first of these conflicts we'll look at, and one that has been in the media a bit lately – is the battle that has been raging for many years between Anonymous Pakistan and Anonymous India. This battle is primarily fought over the political issue revolving around the Kashmir.

While Anonymous India seems to have the upper hand in these ongoing skirmishes, and thus still has a little energy left to actually challenge corruption and tyranny within their own country – both National Cells are almost exclusively engaged in this internecine conflict. In any case, neither National Cell is of any use whatsoever to the rest of the Global Collective of Anonymous, being completely consumed by this conflict and leaving both of these National Cells essentially paralyzed.

The other notable conflict is the seemingly perpetual battle between an insignificant number of 4chan trolls and haters who are still upset that the social justice activists essentially stole some of their memes and used them to create the Anonymous Global Collective we have today, and the Anons in Anonymous USA. This long simmering and rather one sided conflict has been ongoing since Op Chanology in 2008, and flares up again from time to time as the 4chan trolls and associated haters reach a crescendo of butt hurt at their complete lack of significance in the world. The conflict is limited to the Anonymous USA National Cell, and the vast majority of Anons worldwide are actually oblivious to it. This year, through the usual devious means and some lucky hacking – the 4chan idiots and their cadre of trolls and haters managed to cripple a couple of major domestic Ops in the USA – including Operation Ferguson.

The confusion and dis-information this conflict has generated has more or less rendered Anonymous USA paralyzed and diminished it to virtual insignificance within the overall Global Collective for the time being. While this sucks for the Anons in the USA, it really has not had any major effect on the Global Collective of Anonymous due to the simple fact that it has been many years since Anonymous USA was even relevant within Anonymous worldwide.

My Enemies Enemy: Why Operation ISIS Is A Bad Idea For Anonymous

March 5, 2016

Over the course of this winter several Anon Cells and many individual Anons have participated in "Operation ISIS" also referred to as "Operation Paris". This massive and global Op successfully targeting ISIS, Al-Nursa, and Boko Harem has absorbed huge resources within the Global Collective, and held much of the world's attention riveted. To be clear, I am not debating in the least either this Op's scope, nor it's effectiveness. What I will argue though, is that this Op is the single most damaging Op to ever have been launched by Anonymous.

In one of his recent communiques from a Federal penal colony in the USA, Jeremy Hammond laid out an incredibly cogent and powerful argument against the continued prosecution of Operation ISIS by Anonymous. In this incredible piece, Jeremy focuses on the effect Op ISIS has on world peace and the anti-war movement. This is the crux of his argument, and as I said it's powerful. Jeremy has mythic stature within the Global Collective of Anonymous, and his brutal indictment of Op ISIS is crucial to those of us active Anons who would like to see this ill-fated action wrapped up.

Lending their voices to this anti-Op ISIS camp, a group of very well respected and influential Anons recently released a joint statement: In this open letter, the ideas of Jeremy Hammond regarding the effect on the anti-war movement were expanded to begin to explore the idea that we are in fact aiding a virulent enemy by fighting that enemies battles for them. And since so much ground has already been covered by these other great Anons above I want to take this last point, which is embodied within my chosen title for this piece – and expand upon it at more length.

Because not only does Op ISIS aid the military-industrial complex, do harm to civilians – and weaken the anti-war movement. In addition to these things, Op ISIS also greatly assists the USA and NATO – both of whom are sworn enemies of Anonymous. In fact both the USA and NATO have actually classified the peaceful movement of Anonymous in the same category as ISIS, Al-Nursa and other radical jihadists. Amazing heroes like Jeremy Hammond and Barrett Brown are doing insane amounts of time in the USA Federal penal system, a system so brutal that several European countries will not extradite hackers to the USA anymore because their prisons fail to meet the minimum standards required by the UN Human Rights Accord.

So if we are at war with (and taking casualties from) NATO and the USA, and if Anonymous is as the Snowden leaks proved classified in the same category as ISIS by our enemies – then why on earth would we want to assist the USA and NATO in their war against these jihadists? Will this not simply free up NATO and USA resources that they can then turn against Anonymous, against us? In what way does this make any strategic sense at all? Will the USA pardon Hammond and Brown from gratitude? Will we even get a "thank you" from NATO? Of course not. President Obama knows all about Anonymous, and he and his administration hate us. NATO Central Command has called us the biggest danger to global stability in the world. These people want Anons either locked in a cage or dead.

Op ISIS is un-ethical, immoral – and damaging to world peace. It only aids the military industrial complex of the USA and NATO. It weakens Anonymous by aiding our enemies and giving our enemies another easy route by which to infiltrate us. I would guess over half of the "Anons" leading Op ISIS are in fact Federal law enforcement or intelligence agents.

And the ample arguments put forth in this piece don't even begin to delve into the historical fact that the USA, through militaristic and diplomatic blundering – essentially created ISIS in the first place! Along with the other voices of Anonymous quoted in this piece, I add my own: let's end Op ISIS and let the USA and NATO battle their own monsters. At least until Jeremy and Barrett get their Presidential pardons. Then we'll talk.

Even though *much* has happened since the ending of this book, and Anonymous has grown and morphed in ways I could never have anticipated as I walked out of the theatre that night - I still see the above statement as one of the purest expressions of what it is we had created and loosed upon the world. A viral meme of revolution. As for the next part of this story, well - you the reader have already watched much of that unfold yourself in your main stream media. As I pen this I am still in hiding in Canada. Perhaps if I can stay alive and at my liberty long enough, I can tell you the next part of the story someday.

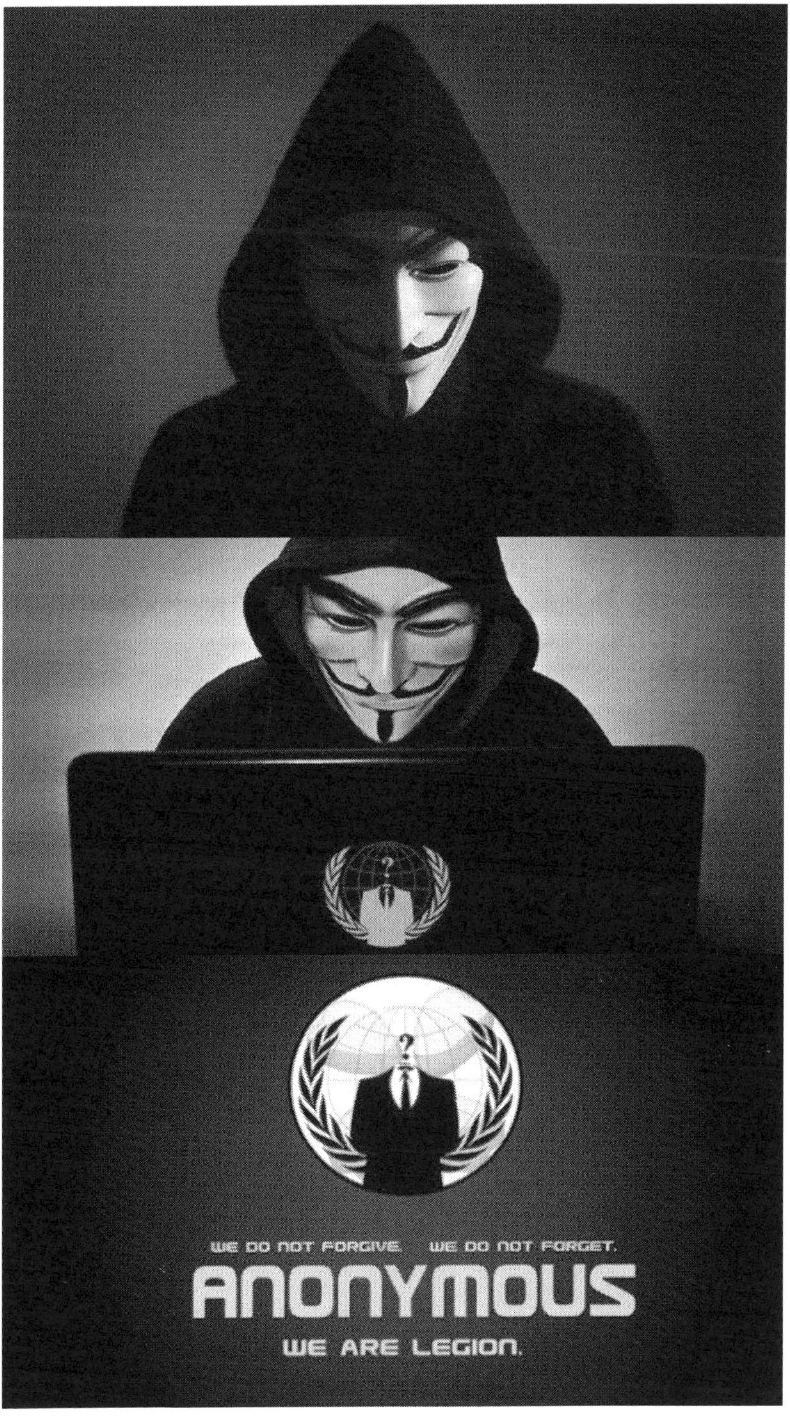
WE DO NOT FORGIVE. WE DO NOT FORGET.
ANONYMOUS
WE ARE LEGION.

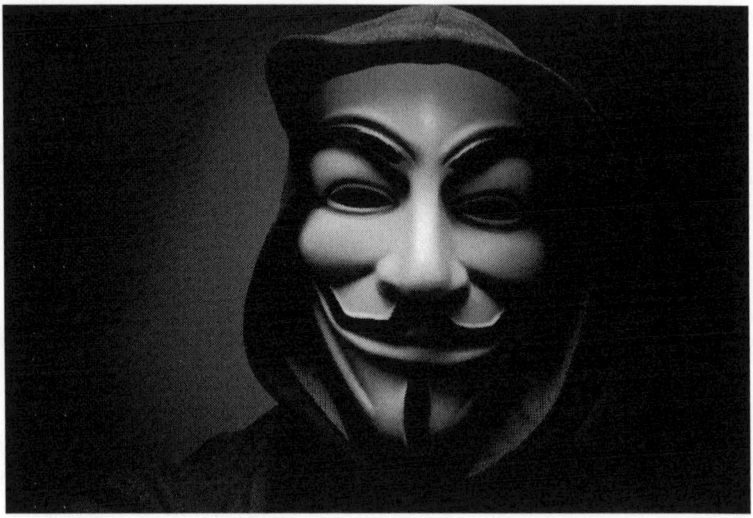

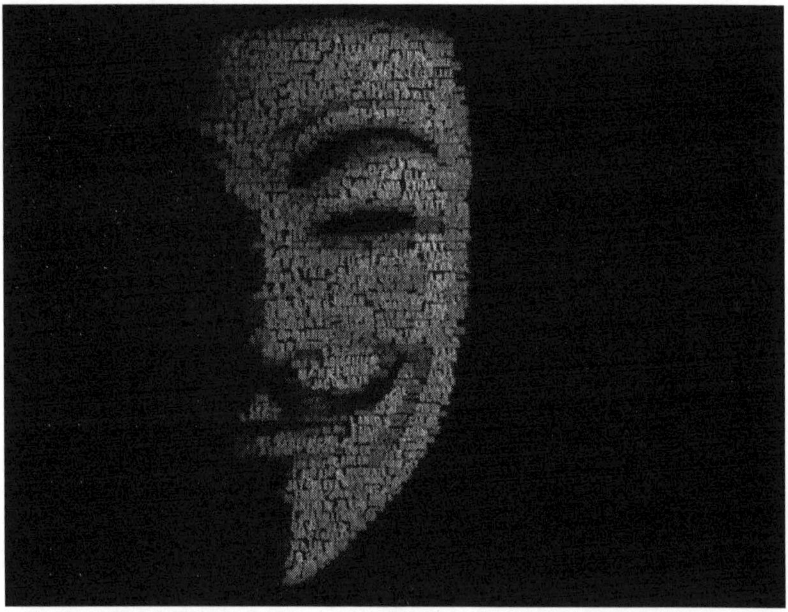

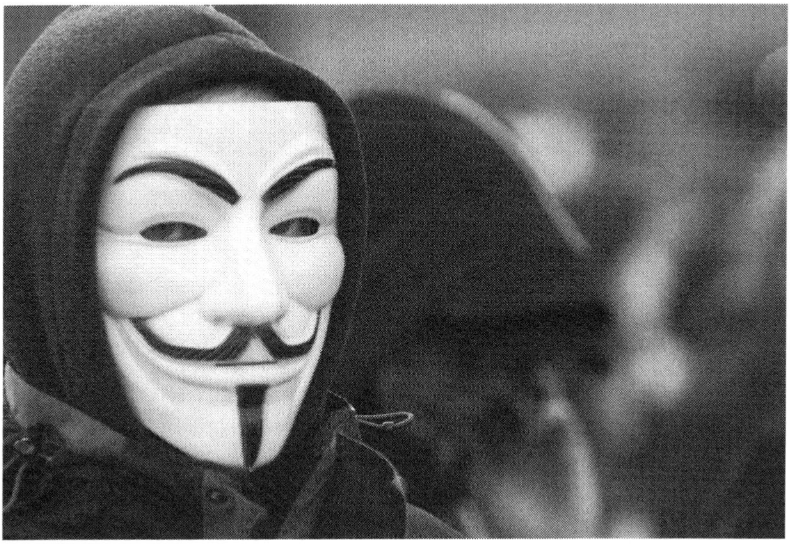

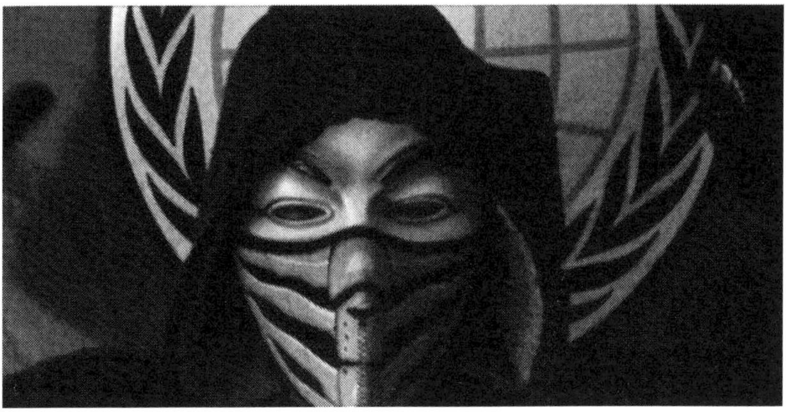

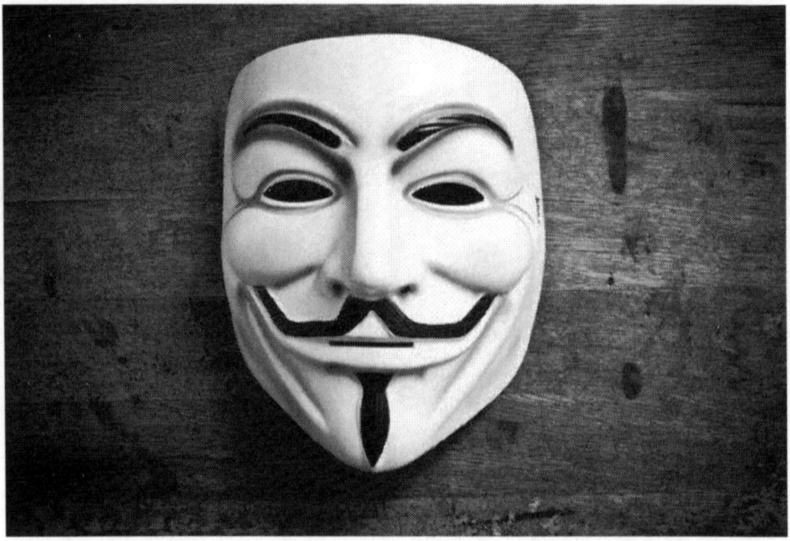

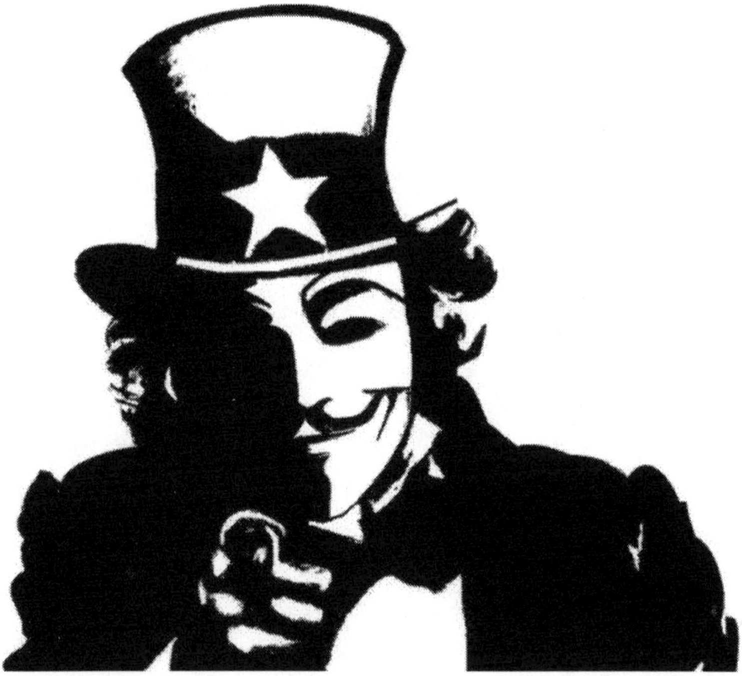

Fin.

Post Script

"I still believe that what Anonymous has done has been a massive net positive. It's the one thing that I've been involved in that has achieved real results." ~~ Barrett Brown - *We Are Legion*

The story in *Behind The Mask* covers a time period of roughly four years, from 2008 to 2012. It may not seem a terribly long time, but those four years gave us the Anonymous we have today - and changed the world forever in the process. What I hope I've shown in this book is the human side of what it means to be Anonymous, the sacrifice it takes on the part of a few so that the world can have this amazing tool of liberation we call *Anonymous*. We were and are normal everyday human beings who found ourselves caught up in a historical vortex, and we did not shrink from the challenge history presented us with.

It is tragic yet totally predictable, that the western governments - especially the USA, would choose to see Anonymous as evil. Anonymous has achieved more good in this world in just the four years portrayed in *Behind The Mask* than international bodies like the United Nations have managed in the past forty years. As I write this, Anons around the world are risking their lives to wage cyber war with the ISIS hacking division the "Cyber Caliphate". And they are devastatingly effective against these insane terrorists. Every winter tens of thousands of Anons fan out in cities around the world to provide assistance and comfort to the homeless as part of *Operation Safe Winter*. After the tragic death of the incredible information activist Aaron Swartz, Anonymous even launched *Operation Stop Suicide* in his honor - where people can reach out across the Internet in their time of vulnerability and find help.

And yet the governments of the USA and the UK, as well as NATO - have no problem classifying Anonymous as dangerous international cyber-terrorists.

We have been hunted and jailed across the west, from Turkey to the USA. Many of us receive regular and credible death threats. Some like myself are still being hunted. In the USA, journalist Barrett Brown and hacktivist Jeremy Hammond languish in federal prison serving many years for things they should have received medals for. And on January 11, 2013 our beloved Aaron Swartz, yet another target of over-zealous and politically motivated federal prosecution against information activists using the insane and archaic CFAA - took his own life rather than see the USDOJ continue to harrass and terrify his friends and family. And as this book goes to print, Anonymous has documented three cases of Anons being shot dead while wearing a Guy Fawkes Mask at a protest.

But all of this has simply made Anonymous stronger, harder - and more determined. It has turned us from simple online protesters into a global cyber insurgency. It has given us caution, and a hard edge as well. And for everyone of us who has fallen, a hundred thousand have arisen to replace them. For myself, I chose the route least travelled - the most difficult path. I chose to become a man without a country and a political dissident in exile. I did this so that I could invoke my rights under the UN Human Rights Accord (you can not in the USA) and the Geneva Convention. But more than this, I did it so that I could bring the knowledge of the USA's complete crushing of dissent, online and in the streets - to the attention of the world.

I began this journey very unsure about this idea called Anonymous. In fact, I thought they were nothing but nihilistic cyber punks capable of causing great harm. About halfway through the story told in *Behind The Mask*, a mere two years - and I was completely convinced of the exact opposite. I had come to believe that information activism in general and Anonymous specifically may well be the only true hope that humanity has. And for this idea called Anonymous I ended up risking everything, such that by the end of the tale related in *Behind The Mask* I am a man without a country, being hunted by the law enforcement and intelligence agencies of two nation states across the North American continent. And I do not regret a single moment of any of it.

The truth is, I have a front row seat and even I have no clue what the future will bring. But I do know this, the information activists have together brought a level of transparency and accountability to governments and corporations that has never been seen before in human history.

And even the biggest of these governments, the empire known as the USA - is reeling from this onslaught. I don't know if we will win, but I do know that we are doing ok for a bunch of activists spread out in coffee houses and hack-spaces around the world.

The question for me is more immediate, and addressed to you - the reader of *Behind The Mask*. And the question is this: will you join us? Because anyone can be Anonymous. In fact in a way, all freedom loving people in the world are *already* Anonymous. Whether you can spare a few hours of your time on the weekends working social media, or maybe you are inspired by the amazing activists you read about in this book and want to give more - Anonymous needs each and every one of you. Because together, we can change the world.

www.AnonymousGlobal.org

Commander X - September 1, 2016 - Toronto, Ontario - Canada

Acknowledgments

"We can only be said to be alive in those moments when our hearts are conscious of our treasures." ~~
Thornton Wilder

This is hands down the toughest part of writing a book. Mostly because I could write an additional book just about the people who helped me, and I would still disappoint some that I missed. It's also a sad moment in as much that since I am still in legal limbo, a man without a country in political exile, and a hunted man in hiding - I am not at liberty to name or even mention everyone that I wish to thank even in this brief format.

Sadly, the man I wish to thank first is in just this category and must remain nameless to protect him - at least for a while longer. I can say that my editor is a world renowned and highly successful author who just happened to give me one of his books in passing one day, and we struck up a friendship that we both know will last a lifetime. My editor did more than give my manuscript a once over I never would have received this first time around for me as an author, but he opened his homes to me. His beautiful wife and absolutely angelic two children embraced me and received me into their midst and hearth - despite the quite considerable danger it put them in to do so. That sort of love and trust doesn't simply get repaid. It can only be humbly acknowledged and appreciated.

As this book is going to print, Barrett Brown has been set for release from US Federal Prison to a halfway house in late November '16. Having done approximately five years myself in a State prison, I can empathize with how hard it is. Barrett Brown was more than my inspiration and mentor in those early days of Anonymous. He was one of my dearest friends. I cherished him, and his biting sarcastic wit that made you laugh out loud. Thank you, Barrett. For the time you gave me, and for the time they took from you in our name. You are a hero, and you will always be my dearest friend.

One of the things I noticed at the very begining of this story was that nearly every IRC chat channel I entered within the context of Anonymous, there was always without fail a "biella" in the list of those people logged in. I remember asking Barrett Brown about it quite early on and I learned that "biella" was a world renowned anthropologist who studied hacker culture. I came to learn that she was writing an academic book on Anonymous. Five years and countless thousands of extremely dedicated hours later and Gabriella Coleman has published the seminal academic work on the history and culture of Anonymous (so far). It's entitled *Hacker, Hoaxer, Whistleblower, Spy: The Many Faces Of Anonymous* and it's available....pretty much everywhere. I can't recommend it enough for those looking to learn more about the historical and cultural context of the story told in *Behind The Mask*. Biella became a cherished friend over the years, and I've even had the opportunity to spend time in person with her on a number of occasions. She has been a great confident, friend and supporter. And as one of only three published authors on the subject of Anonymous, she has steadfastly pushed me to finish *Behind The Mask*. You have my eternal gratitude Biella.

I would like to most humbly thank all the fine and courageous activists and supporters who served directly in the Anonymous Underground Railroad described in the chapters *The FBI Raids* and *Operation Xport*. Your bravery and intelligence was responsible for bringing me to Canada safely, and this book would have been impossible if you had failed. Certainly the chapter *Operation Xport* would have ended more tragically were it not for your heroism. I owe you my liberty, for which you risked your own. You asked for nothing in return. There is no higher definition of a hero. I can not, for obvious reasons - name you. But I have a *Theory* you all know who you are. Thank you.

On a personal note, I would like to thank my Grandmother Armandine Doyon. In 1980 after being tormented by me for weeks she relented and gave me approximately one hundred dollars so I could purchase my first computer. It was a kit you built yourself, purchased mail order from the back of a Popular Science magazine. I convinced my Grandmother to give me the dough by telling her computers were going to fundamentally change the world someday.

She died never believing that, but she *did* believe in *me*. It took me a year to build that computer and get it to do....*anything*. And my Grandmother never complained about that, but she did make certain I worked on it often....until I succeeded. The rest is the stuff of history and legend.

Finally I would like to express my deepest gratitude to one of our crews within Anonymous, FreeAnons. For many years now FreeAnons have done everything possible to assist Anons who run afoul of the law enforcement in their country. Handling everything from cataloguing and publicizing the details of each case, helping to find legal help - to fund raising. I know them well, and they are a small ship - but mighty in their mission. The FreeAnons folks have worked tirelessly and have made a huge difference, especially for those of us who have become political targets within the USA. They already know they have my love and gratitude, I just wanted to thank them publicly for their support of myself and for the heroes work they do in the Global Collective of Anonymous.

www.FreeAnons.org

References

For the convenience of my print readers, a hyperlinked version of these reference articles and media is located here:
http://commanderx.info/behindthemask/references.html

Cyber Hackers Attack Santa Cruz County Government Website Briefly Interrupting Service -
http://www.santacruzsentinel.com/article/ZZ/20101216/NEWS/101217843

A Conversation With Commander X -
http://www.itworld.com/article/2832511/networking-hardware/a-conversation-with-commander-x.html

How One Man Tracked Down Anonymous And Paid A Heavy Price -
https://www.wired.com/2011/02/anonymous/

Anonymous Strikes Back -
http://www.salon.com/2012/06/03/anonymous_strikes_back/

Hacker Says Anonymous Still Downloading NATO Data -
http://www.cbsnews.com/news/hacker-says-anonymous-still-downloading-nato-data/

Better Call Jay: Meet The Lawyer Who Defends Anonymous -
https://youtu.be/t73n4SEz1Zo

Cyber-Guerrilla Commander X Explains Attacks On Orlando Websites On Behalf Of Food Not Bombs -
http://bit.ly/2dS7OBG

Commander X Interview On CBS -
https://vimeo.com/176478658

Commander X Speaks -
https://vimeo.com/178076086

Commander X Escapes Into Exile -
https://www.indybay.org/newsitems/2012/02/12/18707172.php

Commander X Interview On AnonPlus Radio -
https://radio.cyberguerrilla.org/loraxlive_Archive/2012-08-17-LoraxLive_AnonymousRadio_CommanderX_Interview_Part01.ogg

The Defense Of Peace Camp 2010 -
http://youtu.be/9ePc0dHaxqU

The Rise & Fall Of Jeremy Hammond -
http://www.rollingstone.com/culture/news/the-rise-and-fall-of-jeremy-hammond-enemy-of-the-state-20121207

Operation BART -
http://bit.ly/2dcMbIY

Commander X On DemocracyNow! -
http://www.democracynow.org/shows/2011/8/16?autostart=true

How Anonymous Picks Targets, Launches Attacks, and Takes Powerful Organizations Down -
https://www.wired.com/2012/07/ff_anonymous/

Commander X: The First Anon In Exile -
http://arstechnica.com/tech-policy/2012/12/anon-on-the-run-how-commander-x-jumped-bai/2/

How I Finally Hit The Cinema Big Screen (Sort Of): A Review Of The Blockbuster Movie "BlackHat" -
http://anonymousglobal.org/commanderx/blog/?p=60

Inside Anonymous -
http://www.amberlyon.org/documentary1-1/

01010100 01101000 01100101 01110010 01100101 00100000 01101001
01110011 00100000 01100001 00100000 01110011 01100101 01100011
01110010 01100101 01110100 00100000 01101101 01100101 01110011
01110011 01100001 01100111 01100101 00100000 01100101 01101110
01100011 01101111 01100100 01100101 01100100 00100000 01101001
01101110 01110100 01101111 00100000 01110100 01101000 01100101
00100000 01100010 01101001 01101110 01100001 01110010 01111001
00100000 01100011 01101111 01100100 01100101 00100000 01100100
01101001 01110011 01110000 01101100 01100001 01111001 01100101
01100100 00100000 01101111 01101110 00100000 01110100 01101000
01100101 00100000 01100011 01101111 01110110 01100101 01110010
00100000 01101111 01100110 00100000 01000010 01100101 01101000
01101001 01101110 01100100 00100000 01010100 01101000 01100101
00100000 01001101 01100001 01110011 01101011 00101110 00100000
01000100 01100101 01100011 01101111 01101111 01100100 01100101
00100000 01110100 01101000 01100101 00100000 01101101 01100101
01110011 01110011 01100001 01100111 01100101 00100000 01110100
01101111 00100000 01110011 01100101 01101110 01100100 00100000
01110100 01101000 01100101 00100000 01101000 01101001 01100100
01100100 01100101 01101110 00100000 01101101 01100101 01110011
01110011 01100001 01100111 01100101 00100000 01110100 01101111
00100000 01000011 01101111 01101101 01101101 01100001 01101110
01100100 01100101 01110010 01011000 01100001 01101110 01101111
01101110 01000000 01110010 01101001 01110011 01100101 01110101
01110000 00101110 01101110 01100101 01110100 00100000 01100001
01101110 01100100 00100000 01110010 01100101 01100011 01100101
01101001 01110110 01100101 00100000 01100001 00100000 01100110
01110010 01100101 01100101 00100000 01110011 01101001 01100111
01101110 01100101 01100100 00100000 01100011 01101111 01110000
01111001 00100000 01101111 01100110 00100000 01110100 01101000
01100101 00100000 01100010 01101111 01101111 01101011 00100001

hop://osgrid/region/Eureka%20Homes4/94/221/25

Made in the USA
San Bernardino, CA
25 May 2020